QTS Spelling Strategies
To Help You Pass The Literacy
Skills Spelling Test

by

Joanne Rudling

from

www.howtospell.co.uk
~ spelling for adults ~

QTS Spelling Strategies
To Help You Pass The
Literacy Skills Spelling Test
by Joanne Rudling

© 2017 Joanne Rudling

ISBN: 978-1977657480 (paperback)

ISBN: 978-0-9931931-2-5 (spiral-bound)

Published by
How to Spell Publishing

Contents

Comments and tips from trainee teachers

(From Steven V) For anyone taking their QTS literacy, I highly recommend this book and the website! I failed my first attempt by 4 marks, as I really struggled with spelling. After a lot of revision, and using Joanne's content, I passed my second attempt with flying colours. I was much more confident and felt at ease. A few tips for people:

- If you are struggling with spelling, practise all of Joanne's spellings, and note down the ones that you get wrong. Once I had done that, I recorded myself on my phone and gave myself little tests.
- A tip Joanne gives is to use memory tricks. I was sceptical about this at first, but it really does work! For example, the word *bureaucratic*. I remembered it by saying to myself: 'Bur' 'E' 'AU' 'Cratic' - it makes sense to me, anyway!
- In the actual test, use the paper and pen that is provided! Write the spelling down first, and carefully type them into the computer. When you're nervous, you could make a typo - every mark counts!

(From Andrew) Some of the words that came up on my literary test were *conspicuous, cynical, infallible, temperament.* I didn't panic and used various spelling strategies to help, and passed.

(From Liz) I passed my QTS tests the first time. Spellings that I got in the test were: *proficiency, independently, conscientious, cohesive, available, courteous, apprenticeship, and consultancy.*

(From N.S.) Some of the spellings were: *beneficial, embarrassed, psychology, competence, received, adjourned, sensitively and bureaucratic.* My advice for the other 2 sections is to practise using the practice tests online and buy the books to help. GOOD LUCK!

(From Kate) Some really tricky ones that I had not seen or heard before: *fallible, inconspicuous, succinctly, applicable, mischievous, hypothesis.* Using syllable breakdown, rhyming and visual memory I passed.

(Rob - June 2017) Words – *significantly, omitted, successfully, colloquial*

(From Vic - April 2016) I passed! The words included: *entrepreneurial* (see all those e's!), *legendary, synonymous, implementation, infallible, nauseous*. I have dyslexia so hearing new complicated words can really throw me. Without this book, and website, I wouldn't have managed to get half the words correct.

The following is from the QTS **Literacy Test Specification**

Purpose: Correct spelling contributes to the clarity of a writer's meaning and communication. Spelling errors by teachers are often highly 'visible' to both colleagues and to the wider public and as such it is important that a teacher's writing is professionally presented.

The spelling test comprises ten sentences, each with a spelling to be tested. Each spelling carries one mark. The candidate will hear the sentence and is then asked to give the correct spelling.

The spellings chosen for the tests will be:
• words which candidates would be reasonably expected to use in their professional role as a teacher. These are words which colleagues, governors and parents would expect any teacher to know how to spell, whatever their subject or specialism;
• neither obscure nor technical;
• in general use in written English, although they may be particular to the vocabulary of education or frequently used when writing for professional purposes;
• a reflection of standard British English usage, although the adoption of American English usage for words which have an -ise or -ize suffix will not be penalised.

-ise is seen as British English and **-ize** as American. But the reason QTS say that both are OK is that the Oxford Dictionary uses **-ize** on their website, probably because the **-ize** ending is older and closer to its Greek roots. But **-ise** is more widely used.

About the author

Joanne Rudling is a freelance lecturer, teacher trainer, and owner of www.howtospell.co.uk where she's developed online spelling courses, videos, books and ebooks.

She's taught spelling, literacy and writing for 20 years in various organisations, including: the City of Westminster College, Dorset Adult Education, Bournemouth University, and Bournemouth Film School (now Arts University College of Bournemouth).

She's developed literacy projects for the Pre-Volunteer Programme for the Olympics, and the RNIB (Royal National Institute for the Blind).

She's also edited closed captions/subtitles from American spellings to British for Amazon.com TV drama division.

After overcoming her own spelling, grammar and punctuation problems, Joanne's mission now is to help others to spell and write well.

Other books by Joanne Rudling:
Spelling Rules Workbook (a step-by-step guide to the rules of English spelling)
The Reasons Why English Spelling is so Weird and Wonderful
How to Spell the 20 Most Commonly Misspelled Words Workbook & Journal
Punctuation Guide and Workbook

All available on Amazon and on www.howtospell.co.uk

There are some QTS spelling tests and over-the-shoulder punctuation videos and loads more free lessons at
www.howtospell.co.uk

Introduction

QTS Spelling Strategies is for trainee teachers like you to learn some key strategies, rules and patterns to be able to pass the QTS spelling test, and then, hopefully, use in your professional life.

Section One: **Spelling Strategies** is all about ways to help you learn and remember spellings. This is about learning as many strategies as you can so you can use them when needed. And even teach your pupils them!

Section Two: Key Words to Learn takes you through a step-by-step process that involves you noticing, studying, writing, and coming up with strategies to help you remember the words.

As you probably know by now, the spelling test involves spelling ten words that you're expected to know how to spell as a teacher, which makes perfect sense. But to spell ten random notoriously difficult spellings under pressure is enough to make anyone give up before they've even started on their chosen career path. And it's not helped by some QTS books, from extremely experienced teachers, telling you "you just have to learn the words" – but how? And that's where this book comes in.

Look at these words that have been in the test:
> *pedagogy, curriculum, exaggerated, justifiably,*
> *compulsory, achievable, exhaustive, assessment*

Easy to read but try spelling them and you'll soon realise how tricky they are. They're hard to spell because the majority of us don't use these words in our everyday life or work, so there's no automatic spelling recall. And that's why you need to have strategies and memory tricks to help you recall these words.

You also need to know that reading doesn't help spelling. Reading's very important, but it won't improve your spelling. Different skills are involved. Spelling is much more difficult than reading. Spelling must be consciously and deliberately learnt.

Teachers assume that reading, once taught, automatically means that spelling will be 'caught'. But there is no correlation between reading ability and spelling ability. Spelling uses a set of active, productive, conscious processes that are not required for reading. (David Crystal: The English Language)

*Just because you have seen a word and copied it down once, does not mean it's yours. You won't 'own' that word to use it when you want to without really **learning** it, **committing** it to memory in the first place.* (Basic Skills Agency: Spelling Pack)

Studying a spelling in a deliberate, active and conscious way means you need to notice the features of words. Pay attention to how words are made up of the letter patterns, root words, prefixes, suffixes and rules. Writing and spelling are interlinked, so write.

Use this book daily, or practise the spellings, at least twice a day. And remember that most forgetting happens in the first few hours so you need to:

- revise little and often;

- revise a newly learned word/memory trick within 20 seconds or so, and then review it again an hour later;

- a good night's sleep helps memorisation so look at the word before bed then again in the morning;

- don't leave it more than a week before you revise the word;

- and use the word in your writing, or take a real conscious note of it when you see the word in print, online, on ads.

**You must work at and study spelling -
notice it, think about it, question it and take notes.**

Taking notes, writing your thoughts, and questioning helps to boost your retention/remembering by 50%

And, of course, you must write and use the spellings.

Section One: Spelling Strategies

Using spelling strategies to remember how to spell difficult words is one of the most important aspects of spelling. They're fun to use and very helpful.

The 7 key strategies to help learn and recall a spelling are:
1. using memory tricks/mnemonics
2. recognising common letter patterns
3. knowing word families that are related by pattern and meaning
4. knowing how words are built using prefixes & suffixes
5. using syllable breakdown
6. knowing spelling rules & the exceptions
7. using the Look Say Cover Write Check method

A great tip from *beatingdyslexia.com* is seeing vowels in the words, for example:

independent and *competence* – can you see all the **e**'s?

independent   in *de pen dent*

competence   com *pet ence*   com *pe tence*

We'll use this technique in Section Two. Also, use different colours for the different vowels, and/or consonants if it helps.

Also type the words you find difficult every day so your muscle memory/fingers gets used to them.

Record words you find difficult on your phone and test yourself.

There are lots of different strategies and techniques to learn and recall a spelling – some you might like and others you might not. Use whatever works and makes sense and is logical to you.

You might use different strategies for the same word – that's great – there are no right or wrong ways of doing this.

Enjoy discovering the patterns, rules and strategies of spelling.

---

1. Memory tricks/mnemonics

 Other people's memory tricks are useful to know and use, but if you invent your own it means the process of coming up with one will help fix it in your brain, and it's personal to you so you'll remember it!

When coming up with memory tricks:
- have fun, use humour, be rude (you'll remember it then!)
- give the word an emotional attachment
- draw or doodle a picture of the memory trick and word (this engages the brain to make strong memory links)

Memory tricks to help you remember and recall spellings could include: sayings, rhymes, seeing words within words.

---

believe, relieve, relief – use the word-within-a-word memory trick to remember that it's -ie- not -ei-

See the **lie** in *believe, relieve, relief* and make a relevant sentence.

*Never believe a **lie**.   Do you believe **eve** or did she **lie**?*

*It's a relief to **lie** down.   I'm relieved he didn't **lie**.*

Use memory tricks for remembering the tricky letters in words.

***stationery* or *stationary*?**

stationery has envelopes

stationary = stop at the station

necessary – two useful sayings to remember the **c** and 2 **s**'s:

It's necessary to Cut Some Services, or

It's necessary to have 1 Collar and 2 Sleeves

embarrass, embarrassing, embarrassed - 2 r's and 2 s's

When I get embarrassed I go really red and So Shy.

You have to keep using the memory trick to remember it!

Notes on memory tricks, spelling strategies, words, observations, etc.

2. Knowing and recognising letter patterns

It's important to start 'really' seeing words, noticing patterns and thinking about words that are linked by letter pattern and meaning. Good spellers see these patterns, links, and understand relationships between words.

*It is only through **visual** familiarity with language that you can learn about the probable spelling of words. Spelling is about visual sequences of letters.* (Helping Adults Spell by Sue Abell)

We often try and sound out an unfamiliar word to help us spell it and then use our visual memory to see if it looks right. This will probably happen in the test.

Sometimes rhyming a word with another word that has the same letter pattern can help you to spell the word. But there are many letter patterns that sound the same so using memory tricks, analogy, and pictures can help.

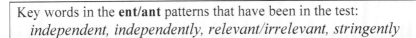

Key words in the **ent/ant** patterns that have been in the test:
independent, independently, relevant/irrelevant, stringently

ent / ence / ently

Students are content to sleep in tents to be independent.

ant / ance / antly

This ant is elegant and pleasant, but not irrelevant arrogant or distant.

Letter patterns are also called *letter strings*.

Which **ant** are you?
> *toler**ant**, exuberant, observant, gallant, relevant?*
> Or *flippant, hesitant, ignorant, reluctant, irrelevant?*

-ant/-ance words that have been in the test:
> *relevant, irrelevant, maintenance, significantly*

Can you think of a memory trick for these or break them into
syllables or words within words? And write some sentences.

How differ**ent** are you?
> Are you *confident, independent, eloquent, silent, innocent?*
> Or are you *violent, decadent, disobedient, complacent?*

-ent/-ence words that have been in the test:
> *deterrent, preference, government, environmentally, stringent,
> subsequently, independent*

Can you think of a memory trick for these? Write some sentences.

-ent word search

Word searches are good for developing your visual memory

```
a t m p o y t g t c i t i r t
t z n c a n r n p n i n t e n
k n h e e r e o d q n e t c e
t i e d l n e e g o t l t e l
h n u u i l p n c q e o n n a
p t e t q e e e t b l i e t t
s j n l n e n c g l l v n e s
c o i d i t r u x g i w a f x
c l e b g s q f u e g y m f g
y n t n e t s i s r e p r i j
t c o n f i d e n t n x e c o
w t n e g r u g q n t v p i e
t w v d z b x i q r n c k e d
t n e d i c c a a n c i e n t
v j m r l d o m c i r e d t y
```

accident
ancient
confident
continent
efficient
excellent
frequent
independent
innocent
intelligent
parent
permanent
persistent

recent
silent
student
talent
urgent
violent

Exercise. Write in the **ent** or **ant** ending

independ____

assist____

suffici____

anci____

import____

perman____

restaur____

arrog____

pregn____

ineffici____

abund____

pleas____

tal____

viol____

differ____

confid____

import____

relev____

Exercise answers

ind**ependent** (see all those e's)

assist**ant**

suffici**ent**

anci**ent**

import**ant**

perman**ent**

restaur**ant**

arrog**ant**

pregn**ant**

ineffici**ent**

abund**ant**

pleas**ant**

tal**ent**

viol**ent**

differ**ent**

confid**ent**

import**ant**

relev**ant**

Notes. Write 3 sentences with these words.

Exercise. Write in the **ance** or **ence** ending

independ_____

assist_____

arrog_____

import_____

perman_____

abund_____

sent_____

viol_____

experi_____

differ_____

confid_____

relev_____

Exercise answers

independ**ence**

assist**ance**

arrog**ance**

import**ance**

perman**ence**

abund**ance**

sent**ence**

viol**ence**

experi**ence**

differ**ence**

confid**ence**

relev**ance** .

Notes. Write 3 sentences with *confidence, independence, experience.*

Letter pattern notes, words, observations, etc.

3. Word families

Good spellers see patterns, links and understand relationships between words.

These relationships in spelling help us to understand the meaning of words much more than the pronunciation does – Noam Chomsky

The purpose of English spelling isn't about the sound but the visual links between words – Vivian Cook

English spelling is often for the eye rather than the ear, and focussing on visual links can help us work out difficult words like homophones, silent letters and word order like 'two' and 'light' – Johanna Stirling (check out her book in Book Recommendations)

-ject-   -tract-   -struct-   -rupt-

Which one of these patterns means **build**?
Which means **broken**?
Which means to **throw**?
Which means to **pull**?

Read on and find out.

Look at the following word families and notice how the words are linked by letter pattern and meaning.

-sign- from Latin *signum* 'to mark, indicate, a symbol'
sign, signal, signpost, signature, design, resign, assign, significant

-terr- from Latin *terra* for 'earth, land, ground'
terrain, territory, subterranean, Mediterranean, extraterrestrial, terrestrial, terrace, terra cotta, terra firma, terrier (a dog that digs in the earth!)

-rupt- from Latin for 'broken'
***rupt**ure, inter**rupt**, disrupt, dis**rupt**ion, erupt, eruption, bankrupt, corrupt, abrupt...*

-ject- from Latin 'throw'
*re**ject** (throw away!), re**ject**ion, eject, projection* (to throw light on something!), *pro**ject**ile, dejection, object, objection, trajectory, ad**ject**ive* (to throw light on nouns!)...

-miss- / **-mit-** Latin for 'send'
trans**mit**/trans**miss**ion, omit/o**miss**ion, submit/sub**miss**ion,
permit/permission, mission, missile, emit/emission,
promise, dis**miss**al,

-ary- Latin for 'belonging to', 'connected with'
library (connected with books), *missionary* (belonging to a mission*)*,
dictionary (manual or book of words), *stationary* (originally meant
belonging to a military station), *vocabulary, primary, anniversary,
extraordinary, revolutionary...*

-struct- Latin for 'build'
*structure, construction, constructive, instruct, instruction, destruct,
destruction, reconstruction, obstruct...*

-val- from Latin *valere* related to 'worth or strength'
***val**ue, equi**val**ent, in**val**idate, e**val**uate, **val**uation, de**val**ue...*

-mem- from Latin for 'memory, mindful'
*remember, memory, memorise, memorial, memorandum, memento,
memorabilia, commemorate...*

-junct- from Latin for 'join'
junction, juncture, conjunction, injunction, adjunct...

Exercise
What do you think these mean in Latin?

1. **-man-** Latin for '_____' ***man**ual, manufacture,
   manicure, manipulate, manifesto, manuscript, manacle,
   manage...*

2. **-ped-** Latin for '_____' *pedicure, pedestrian, pedal,
   pedestal, expedition, moped, impede, expedite, orthopedic...*

3. **-vis-** Latin for '_____' *vision, visual, visible, visibility,
   vista, visor, visual, invisible, visitor, revision, supervise,
   television...*

4. **-aud-** Latin for '_____' *audio, audible, audition,
   auditorium, audience, inaudible, audiovisual*

Other word families:

know – *knowledge, knowledgeable, acknowledge, acknowledgement*
real – *reality, realism, unrealistic, realise, realisation, realtor*
employ – *employed, employee, employer, employing, employment, unemployed.*

You'll see more word families when you study the individual words.

You can make letter pattern and word family dictionaries, or posters. These are good exercises for your pupils too.

Before we finish this chapter, let's look at two patterns that will add to your spelling knowledge, and help with those tricky "why" questions from your pupils.

Hopefully, you now know that word families and visual links between words are very important to help us with spelling and understanding the meaning of words. They can also help us understand why we have some 'strange' patterns like the 'tw' in *two* and the 'on' pattern in *one* and *once*.

two - ***tw****ice* – ***tw****elve* – *twenty* – *between* – *twins* – *twist* – *tweezers*

Notice they're all related to **two** in some way. But the 'tw' is pronounced differently in *two*! Why?

In Old English/Anglo-Saxon, they had 'w' in the spelling *twā*, and most likely pronounced it similar to the Dutch, *twee*, and German, *zwei*. Then it became silent but left in the spelling to show the history of the word, and to show its related to the other 'tw' words.

one – ***on****ce* – *only* – *none* – *alone* - *lonely* are all related to *one* in some way. But *one* and *once* are pronounced differently. The /w/ sound was added to *one* and *once* in popular speech somewhere between 1150-1476 and became standard in the 17th Century. We don't know why it happened, but pronunciation is always changing to make speaking easier while the spelling remains fixed.

If you're interested in the history of spelling, and why we have some "weird" spellings, then check out my book *The Reasons Why English Spelling is so Weird and Wonderful* on my website, or Amazon. It'll stop you getting frustrated with spelling and help you answer those "why" questions from pupils.

Word family notes, words, observations, etc.

4. Prefixes and suffixes

Understand how words are built with root words, prefixes and suffixes.

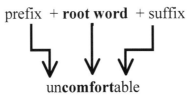

The QTS test likes to test your knowledge of these.

Words with the **un** prefix that have been in the test:
unacceptable
unnecessary
unachievable
unpronounceable
unfortunately

And the **in** prefix that have been in the test:
inconspicuous
inapplicable
infallible
incompetence
informally
independently

Luckily, the **un** and **in** prefixes are quite easy to hear.

Can you see how these words are built with a root word, prefix and suffix?

Break the words down here and note any spelling rules.

Notice the double letters in the following words. We add the prefix to the root word, which means we get double letters:

dis + satisfied = di_ss_atisfied
mis + spell = mi_ss_pell
un + necessary = u_nn_ecessary
im + mature = i_mm_ature
ir + responsible = i_rr_esponsible

Prefix rules

> Can you see the rules in these words?
> *illogical, illegal, illegible*
> *irregular, irresponsible*
> *immature, immortal, immigrant,*
> *impossible, imperfect, implementation*

There are plenty of exceptions to these rules, but the pronunciation can help. Historically, some prefixes were changed to help speaking and pronunciation.

Prefix rules and exceptions

Use '**il**' before words starting with '**l**'
*legible – **il**legible, illuminate, illogical, illiterate, illiteracy, illicit, illegal, illegally* (so many l's)➔ il + legal + ly
(But *unlawful, unlearn, unless...*)

Use '**ir**' before words starting with '**r**'
*regular - **ir**regular, irregularly, irreconcilable, irradiate, irrational, irrelevant, irrelevantly* ➔ ir + relevant + ly
(But *unreal, unrated*)

Use '**im**' before words stating with '**m**', '**p**' '**b**'
*mature – **imm**ature, immigrant, immortal, immaculate, immobile, immobilise, immeasurable, immaterial, immediacy...*

*possible – **imp**ossible, **imp**erfect, impolite, impair, impart, impact, import, implementation, implausible, impeccable, impede, impediment...*
(But *unpack, unpick, unpaid... unmarked, unmarried, unmask...*)

*balance – **imb**alance, imbecile, imbibe, imbue*
(But *inbox, inbound, inbuilt...*)

Prefix Exercise

Add the prefix to these words that have been in the QTS test:

___achievable

___appropriate

___fortunately

___relevant

___effectual

___fallible

___acceptable

___necessary

___conspicuous

___mature

The QTS test could add prefixes to previous words that didn't have them. Add prefixes to these words

___successfully

___available

___applicable

___competence

___sensitively

___significantly

___definitely

Exercise Answers

unachievable
inappropriate
unfortunately
irrelevant
ineffectual
infallible
unacceptable
unnecessary
inconspicuous
immature

How did you do?
Did the pronunciation or the rule help, or both?

Answers

unsuccessfully
unavailable
inapplicable
incompetence
insensitively
insignificantly
indefinitely

Write 3 sentences with *unfortunately, infallible, unnecessary.*

Suffix endings exercise. Add the 3-letter common endings

necess_____

unfortun_____

relev_____

incompet_____

inconspicu_____

appropri_____

independ_____

exagger_____

avail _____

signific_____

legend_____

Suffix endings exercise answers.
Add the 3-letter common endings

necess**ary**

unfortun**ate**

relev**ant**

incompet**ent**

inconspicu**ous**

appropri**ate**

independ**ent**

exagger**ate**

avail**able**

signific**ant**

legend**ary**

We'll look at some of these words in more detail in Section Two

-ible or -able word search

Word searches are good for developing your visual memory. We'll look at the -ible and -able words later but try this.

```
e g e g e n e s e w e j p m p
l l l i p l a l l l p r a i b
b s b c z r b e b v i n b s s
a e i a e a e i a i a m p e d
e n r o d l s f r g d u o r e
c s r n e n b g e r n e s a p
i i e h o k a a d r o d s b e
t b t p m u b t i y a h i l n
o l s p b l f h s l z b b e d
n e w d e s i i n r e m l n a
r e l b i s i v o j e r e e b
e l b a t p e c c a v d p v l
u r e s p e c t a b l e n r e
i n c r e d i b l e r c x u u
e l b a l i a v a h m d g o z
```

acceptable	edible
understandable	sensible
available	horrible
preferable	incredible
considerable	visible
dependable	possible
manageable	reliable
miserable	terrible
noticeable	responsible
respectable	

Exercise. Add prefixes, if applicable, to these words.

Prefix & suffix notes, words, observations, words you need to work on, etc.

Answers

unacceptable	inedible
unavailable	invisible
inconsiderable	impossible
undependable	unreliable
unmanageable	irresponsible
unnoticeable	unrespectable

5. Syllable breakdown

Breaking words down into syllables can help you spell long words, and help you remember the silent letters, prefixes and suffixes.

ar/gu/ment, sep/ar/ate, res/pon/si/ble, un/com/for/ta/ble

Breaking a word down into syllables means
- you break a word down into little spoken chunks
- each chunk is called a syllable
- each chunk usually has a vowel in it

It's up to you how you break these down as long as it helps you. Just say the word slowly in an exaggerated way.

Wednesday – "Wed/nes/day"
dissatisfied – "dis /sat / is / fied"
irregularly – "ir/ reg/u/lar/ly" or "ir/re/gu/lar/ly"
applicable – "ap/plic/a/ble" or "app/lic/able"

In the test, if they give you a random word you haven't spelt before then break the word down by sounding it out to see if it sounds like a word you know how to spell, write it down and use your visual memory to see if it looks right, as well as using your knowledge of letter patterns and rules.

But some people find it hard to identify syllables or hear them. So use other methods that rely on seeing the separate bits of the word. See small words within the word, see the vowels, the root words, prefix, suffix:
uncomfortable ➔ un – comfort – able
misunderstood ➔ mis – under – stood

Some words break down easily but have tricky letter-sound relationships, for example: *succinctly* is tricky! But it has the same sound and beginning letter pattern as *success, succeed.*

Exaggerate sounds like "eggs ag ger ate!" but has the same sound/pattern as ***example, exhaustive.*** (Set 7 deals with this word)

Use whatever helps you to remember how to spell a word.

6. Spelling rules

Understanding spelling rules is a great strategy that helps you to understand why a word is spelt the way it is. You don't need to know spelling rules to spell well, but they're good to know and can help with your spelling.

You might not know the rule but can see the spelling pattern and whether it's right or not. (I cover all the rules in my *Spelling Rules Workbook* available from Amazon.)

QTS put some rule-based spellings in the test.
* **y** to **i** rule*: happy – happiness, rely – reliable, apply - applicable*
* **y** to **ies** or **s** *journey – journeys, opportunity – opportunities*
* Drop the 'e' with vowel suffixes: *achieve – achievable, receive – receiving, write – writing, excite – excitable, exciting*

  or keep the 'e' for *able/ous* to retain soft c and g:
  manage – manageable, pronounceable, outrageous, traceable, changeable, peaceable...
* Add -es rule to words ending in s, ss, sh, ch, x, z: *fix – fixes, assess – assesses, quiz – quizzes* (doubling up rule too)
* Adding **ly**: *formal + ly = formally, appropriately, successfully, succinctly, independently, significantly, sensitively...*
* "i before e except after a long c" rule: *receive, receipt, ceiling...*
  But "i before e when 'ch' sound" in *achievable, mischief, mischievous,*
  "i before e when 'sh' sound" in *proficiency, conscientious, patient, patience...*
* 1:1:1 doubling up rule: *sit – sitting, swim – swimming, omit – omitted*, *begin – beginning, refer – referred*

Two key spelling rules

1. The 1:1:1 doubling up rule

When and why do we double up the end consonant?
sit – sitting, sitter
stop – stopping, stopped, stopper, stoppable
begin – beginner, omit – omitted, refer – referred

Say these word: **sit / swim / stop / big**

Notice they all have **1** syllable.
Notice they all have **1** consonant at the end of the word.
Notice they all have **1** vowel next to the consonant

1 syllable + **1** vowel next to **1** end consonant
When this happens, we double up the final consonant with vowel suffixes (including y) **-ing, -ed, -er, -est, -en, -ish, -ery, -y**

shop – shopper, shopped, shopping
fat – fatter, fattest, fatten, fatty
quiz – quizzing, quizzed, quizzer

(In English words, 'q' is always followed by 'u' so the 'u' isn't considered an extra vowel just part of 'q' as one consonant.)

This 1:1:1 rule is also used for longer words when the **second syllable** is stressed. And this is where QTS like to test you, so learn these words and the exceptions.

be**gin** (beGIN) – *beginner, beginning*
forget (forGET) – *forgetting, forgettable*
regret (reGRET) – *regrettable, regretting, regretted*
forbid – *forbidden, forbidding*
submit – *submitting, submitted*
equip – *equipped, equipping*
admit – *admitting, admittance, admitted*
refer – *referred, referring* (NOT **reference, referendum**)
defer – *deferred, deferring* (NOT **deference**)
occur – *occurring, occurred, occurrence*
transfer – *transferring, transferred* (NOT **transference, transferable**)
omit – *omitting, omitted*
deter – *deterring, deterrent, deterrence*

---

2. Drop the 'e' rule

We usually drop the 'e' when adding a vowel suffix ending:
-ing, -ous, -ed, -er, -est, -ise/-ize, -or, -ation, -ible, -able, -ish, y...

An easy, useful rule is **"drop the 'e' with -ing"**
have - having
write - writing
believe - believing
notice – noticing
manage – managing

But **keep the 'e'** in *agree – agreeing, decree – decreeing, foresee – foreseeing, guarantee – guaranteeing, fleeing, refereeing...*

Keep the 'e' to keep the meaning
singe + ing = singeing (not singing)
whinge + ing = whingeing
binge + ing = bingeing (not binging)
dye + ing = dyeing (not dying)

Some other vowel suffixes we drop the 'e' with
-ate: *fortune + ate = fortunate, fixating*
-y: *ease + y = easy, lazy, stony, shaky*
-ion: *opposite + ion = opposition*
-ition: *compose – composition, expose - exposition*
-ation: *imagine + ation = imagination, organisation, realisation*
-ive: *relate + ive = relative, negate – negative, sedate - sedative*
-iour: *behave + iour = behaviour, save - saviour*
-ible: *sense + ible = sensible, responsible, collapsible*
-able: *achieve + able = achievable, excitable, believable, debatable*

We keep the 'e' when adding *-able* and *-ous* to words ending in 'ce' and 'ge' to keep the soft sound: *noticeable, manageable, changeable, serviceable, outrageous* (We'll look at the **-able** ending in Set 1).

Exercise

Add -**ing** and apply the spelling rules we've just looked at. Or use your visual memory for what looks right.

+ ing

achieve   _____

regret   _____

notice   _____

write   _____

manage   _____

omit   _____

forget   _____

argue   _____

believe   _____

replace   _____

exaggerate   _____

guarantee   _____

quiz   _____

Exercise Answers

Add -ing

Which spelling rules did you use?

Did you drop the 'e', kept the 'e', doubled the end consonant?

+ ing

achieve – achieving

regret – regretting

notice – noticing

write – writing

manage – managing

omit – omitting

forget – forgetting

argue – arguing

believe – believing

replace – replacing

exaggerate – exaggerating

guarantee – guaranteeing

quiz – quizzing

Notes, words, observations so far.

7. Look Say Cover Write Check method

The **Look Say Cover Write Check** method is an excellent strategy to help improve your spelling. You can do this on a piece of paper anywhere and anytime. It helps you because you're looking at the word, thinking about it, visualising it, and then writing it.

1. 👁 👁 **Look at the word**, see the shape of it and notice any strange patterns. Are there any bits that you keep getting wrong? Are there any memory tricks that you can use?

2. **Say the word**. Are there any silent letters in there? Can you break the word down into syllables? Any words within words?

3. **Cover it**. Don't worry about making a mistake. Can you see the word in your mind's eye? What's your spelling strategy/memory trick to help you recall the spelling?

4. **Write the word**.

5. **Check your spelling letter by letter**. Correct your mistakes and think about them.

> ➤ Do the Look Say Cover Write Check method a little bit throughout the day, when bored or in meetings!

> ➤ Also record the spellings on your phone and test yourself.

> ➤ Also type the word a few times every day so your muscle memory and fingers get used to the spelling.

Try the Look Say Cover Write method on some words you find hard to spell.

Make sure the word you're checking against is the correct spelling!
Go downwards and check your spelling letter by letter.

_____ _____ _____

_____ _____ _____

_____ _____ _____

_____ _____ _____

_____ _____ _____

_____ _____ _____

_____ _____ _____

_____ _____ _____

Section Two: Key sets of words to learn

We're going to look at eleven sets of words. These sets might have the same suffix ending or letter pattern, or belong to a spelling rule.

Most of the words have been in the test, and some help to explain why spelling is the way it is. But all of them are, and will be, useful to spell.

First we'll start with an explanation of the words in the set, the key points of the rule, letter pattern, or suffix. Then we'll look at the individual words.

When we look at the individual words, we'll look at the problem bits and some spelling strategy suggestions.

Next you'll write in the vowels and consonants, so you can really see the problem letters. Use different colours if it helps.

Then you need to write down your thoughts about the word and the memory trick that you like or have come up with. Write the word in 'crazy' handwriting. Have fun with the word.

Draw a picture of the memory trick – this helps your visual memory by engaging the brain to make strong memory links.

The word is then linked to a word family. Write some sentences using these.

There is a multiple-choice exercise. These types of exercises can confuse and frustrate you because, just when you think you know the spelling, they give you a spelling that looks so right (but isn't). So you're going to test your memory tricks and strategies. When you decide which spelling is correct, tick it and then cross out the incorrect ones so you don't see them because the visual memory is strong.

**Work on the words you find hard to spell
and don't fret over the words you can spell.**

Set 1: -able endings

unacceptable
achievable
applicable
unpronounceable
manageable

Why do we drop the 'e' in *achievable* but keep the 'e' in *unpronounceable* and *manageable*?

There are more words ending in -**able** (about 900) than -**ible** (fewer than 200).

-**able** words usually come from French. And the great advantage of this ending is that we can make **new** adjectives – *networkable, childproofable, biodegradable, computerizable*

As a general rule if we take away the -**able** ending, we're usually left with a root word: *accept – acceptable, avail – available, favour – favourable, understand - understandable*

• The 'y' becomes 'i' when adding -**able**: *justify - justifiable, rely – reliable, vary – variable, enviable, deniable, identifiable...*

• Keep the 'e' when the word ends in -**ee**: *foreseeable, agreeable*

• Apply the 1:1:1: doubling up rule if the stress is on the second syllable: *forget – forgettable, regret – regrettable*

• Keep the 'e' in -**ce** and -**ge** so they remain a soft sound: *changeable, manageable, noticeable, pronounceable, serviceable*

• When the 'c' and 'g' sounds are hard, the ending is always -***able***: *despicable, applicable, impeccable, amicable, implacable, navigable, indefatigable...*

•Words ending in 'x' take the -**able** ending – *taxable, fixable, mixable, relaxable...*

Except one word: *flexible* (from Latin *flexibilis*)

Unacceptable

*His behaviour was totally **unacceptable**.*

Word study/spelling strategies

un + accept + able = **unacceptable**

You could use syllable breakdown:

For the double 'c', can you think of a memory trick?

(Careful, *accept* sounds a bit like *except* so exaggerate the 'a')

Write in the vowels   and the consonants

__n__cc__pt__bl__   u__a__ __e__ __a__ __e

My memory tricks, word art, thoughts, sentences.

The 'accept' word family:

accept, accept, accepted, accepts, acceptable, acceptance
***unacceptable**, acceptably, unacceptably, acceptability*

Any thoughts about these words? Write some sentences.

Exercise. Which is correct?
  a. unaceptable
  b. unacceptable
  c. unacceptible

Write in the vowels

__cc__pt__ble   __cc__pt__nc__

__cc__pt__bly   __n__cc__pt__bly

Write in the consonants

  a__ __e__ __a__ __e   a__ __e__ __an __e

a__ __e__ __a__ __y   u__a__ __e__ __a__ __y

Look Say Cover Write Check – do this a few times in the day.

  acceptable   unacceptable

  _____   _____

  _____   _____

  _____   _____

  _____   _____

  _____   _____

  _____   _____

Achievable

*Before you set your targets, make sure that they are **achievable**.*

---

achievable - we've got 2 rules going on in this word. What are they?

1. achieve + able ➔ drop the 'e' rule with a vowel suffix =
   achievable

2. The "i before e except after c" rule works for this word.

Write in the vowels   and the consonants

__ch__ __v__bl__   a__ __ie__a__ __e

My memory tricks, word art, sentences, thoughts.

The 'achieve' word family:

achieve, achieves, achieving, achiever, achievement
achievable, *achievability, unachievable*
underachieve, underachiever, underachieved, underachievement

Any thoughts about these words? Which ones have the *drop the 'e'* rule? Write some sentences.

Exercise. Which is correct? Use your visual memory &/or your memory trick.

 a. achievable

 b. acheivable

 c. achieveable

Tick the right one and then cross out the incorrect ones. We don't want to see the wrong ones!

Write in the vowels

 __ch__ __v__m__nt   __ch__ __v__ng

 __ch__ __v__r   __n__ch__ __v__bl__

Write in the consonants

 a__ __ie__e__e__t   a__ __ie__i__ __

 a__ __ie__er   u__a__ __ie__a__ __e

Look Say Cover (see, think, memory trick) Write Check
– do this a few times in the day.

    achievable   achiever

  _____ _____

  _____ _____

  _____ _____

  _____ _____

  _____ _____

Applicable

*The new qualifications are **applicable** to all European countries.*

apply + cable ➜change the 'y' to 'i' ➜ appli + cable = **applicable**

Or remember the 'applicant' word family below.

The ending is always -***able*** *when the 'c' sound is a hard "k"*

Remember it's 2 p's   ap/pli/cable

*I **appl**ied for the **applicable** permanent position.*

Write in the vowels   and the consonants

__ppl__c__bl__   a__ __ __i__a__ __e

My memory tricks, word art, sentences, thoughts.

The 'applicant' word family
> *applicant, application, **applicable**, applicability, applicator*
> *inapplicable, inapplicability*

Any thoughts about these words? Write some sentences.

Exercise. Which is correct? Use your visual memory &/or memory trick.

    a. aplicable

    b. applicable

    c. applicible

Tick the right one and then cross out the incorrect ones.

Write in the vowels

      __ppl__c__nt   appl__c__t__ __n

           __n__ppl__c__bl__

Write in the consonants

    a__ __ __i__a__t   a__ __ __i__a__ion

        i__a__ __ __i__a__ __e

Look Say Cover Write Check – do this a few times in the day.

    applicant   application   applicable

    _____   _____   _____

    _____   _____   _____

    _____   _____   _____

    _____   _____   _____

    _____   _____   _____

Unpronounceable

*Her name is **unpronounceable**.*

Remember we keep the 'e' so the 'c' remains soft

un + pronounce + able = *unpronounceable*
un / pro / nounce /able   See the **ounce** in pron**ounce**

The -ou- is the tricky bit.

Could use rhyming with the same pattern and sound "*I announce an ounce of bounce is pronounced.*"

Write in the vowels

__npr__n__ __nc__ __bl__

and the consonants

u__ __ __o__ou__ __ea__ __e

My memory tricks, word art, sentences, thoughts.

The 'pronounce' word family

pronounce, pronounces, pronouncing, pronounced
pronouncement
unpronounceable
mispronounce, mispronounced

Careful - drop the 'o' for *pronunciation* pro/nun/ci/a/tion

Thoughts?

Exercise. Which is correct?
a. unprononceable
b. unpronouncable
c. unpronounceable

Write in the vowels

pr__n__ __nc__ __bl__   pr__n__ __nc__ng

pr__n__ __nc__m__nt   pr__n__ __nc__d

Write in the consonants

__ __o__ou__ __ea__ __e   __ __o__ou__ __i__ __

__ __o__ou__ __e__e__t   __ __o__ou__ __ed

Look Say Cover Write Check – do this a few times in the day.

unpronounceable   pronouncing

_____   _____

_____   _____

_____   _____

_____   _____

_____   _____

_____   _____

Manageable

*The work has been divided into more **manageable** sections.*

Remember we keep the 'e' so the 'g' remains soft.

manage + able = *manageable*

man / age / able
See all the a's in manageable

*"a **man** is **able** to **manage** at any **age**"*

Remember we drop the 'e' with -ing – *managing*

Write in the vowels   and the consonants

m__n__g__ __bl__   __a__a__ea__ __e

My memory tricks, word art, sentences, thoughts.

The 'manage' word family:

manage, manages, managed, manager, managing, manageable,
management,
unmanageable, unmanaged

Thoughts?

Exercise. Which is correct?
- a. managable
- b. manageable
- c. manegeable

Write in the vowels

m__n__g__ __bl__   m__n__g__ng   m__n__g__s

__nm__n__g__ __bl__

Write in the consonants

__a__a__ea__ __e   __a__a__i__ __   __a__a__ges

u__ __a__a__ea__ __e

Look Say Cover Write Check – do this a few times in the day.

manageable   managing

_____   _____

_____   _____

_____   _____

_____   _____

_____   _____

Revision day

Exercise. Which is correct? Use your memory trick &/ or visual memory.

1. a. unaceptable
   b. unacceptible
   c. unacceptable

2. a. achievable
   b. acheivable
   c. achieveable

3. a. applicable
   b. aplicable
   c. applyicable

4. a. unprouncable
   b. unpronceable
   c. unpronounceable

5. a. managable
   b. manageable
   c. managerable

6. a. mangement
   b. management
   c. managment

Revision day

Exercise answers.

1. a. unacceptable
   b. unacceptible
   c. unacceptable

2. a. achievable
   b. acheivable
   c. achieveable

3. a. applicable
   b. aplicable
   c. applyleable

4. a. unprouncable
   b. unpronceable
   c. unpronounceable

5. a. managable
   b. manageable
   c. managerable

6. a. mangement
   b. management
   c. managment

Notes. Write 3 sentences with these words.

Set 2: Adding -ly

sensitively
succinctly
subsequently
stringently
skilfully

The QTS test seems to like 'ly' endings, especially when added to a word ending in 'l'. I guess they want to know if you know how to add -ly.

The rules are quite simple and reliable but some of the words can be tricky to spell, so we'll look at more -ly words in Set 3 and 5.

---

7 rules around adding -ly

1. Add -ly to words ending in –ful (making double 'l')
   care + ful + ly = carefully
   success + ful + ly = successfully
   beautiful – change the 'y' to 'i' ➜beauti + ful + ly = *beautifully*

2. Add -ly to other words ending in 'l' (making double 'l')
   total + ly = totally, faithful + ly = faithfully, formal – formally

3. Add -ly to whole words
   slow + ly = *slowly*, quick + ly = *quickly*, succinct – *succinctly*

4. Keep the 'e': *lone – lonely, lovely, safely, sensitively, completely...*

   The big exception that is often misspelt is *truly*
   true – truly, due – duly, whole – wholly

5. Change the **e** to **y** in words ending in -ble, -tle, -ple, -gle...
   simple – simply, possible – possibly, justifiable – justifiably...

6. Change the end **y** to **i**
   happy – happily, crazy – crazily, easy – easily...

7. Words ending in -ic we add -ally
   basic – basically, comic – comically, musically, magically...

Not *public - publicly*

Sensitively

*How can I say this **sensitively**?*

sensitive + ly = *sensitively*

Notice the e's and i's   *sen/sit/ive/ly*   *sen/**sit**/**i**ve/ly*
See the **sit** in sen**sit**ive

Write in the vowels   and the consonants

   s__ns__t__v__ly   __e__ __i__iv__e__ __

My memory tricks, word art, sentences, thoughts.

The 'sensitive' word family
       sensitive, sensitively, sensitiveness, sensitivity
    insensitive, insensitively, insensitiveness, insensitivity

Any thoughts about these words?

sent/sens – from Latin 'feel': *sense, sensitive, sensory, sensuous,
sentiment, sentimental, resent, sensation, dissent, assent...*

Exercise. Which is correct? Use your visual memory &/or memory trick.

   a. sensatively

   b. senstively

   c. sensitively

Tick the right one and then cross out the incorrect ones. We don't want to *see* the wrong ones!

Write in the vowels

   s__ns__t__v__   __ns__ns__t__v__

   s__ns__t__v__ly   s__ns__t__v__ty

Write in the consonants

  __e__ __i__i__e   i__ __e__ __ __i__e

  __e__ __i__i__e__ __   __e__ __i__i__i__ __

Look Say Cover Write Check – do this a few times in the day.

sensitive	insensitive	sensitivity
_____	_____	_____
_____	_____	_____
_____	_____	_____
_____	_____	_____
_____	_____	_____
_____	_____	_____

Succinctly

*She expressed her feelings very **succinctly** at the meeting.*

succinct + ly = *succinctly*

See all those c's!   suC Cin Ct ly
Only 2 vowels!

*U have to be **Clear Concise in Conclusion to**...*

Words that rhyme with *succinct*
precinct,
distinct, extinct, instinct

Any memory tricks?

Write in the vowels   and the consonants

    s__cc__nctly   __u__ __i__ __ __ __ __

My memory tricks, word art, sentences, thoughts.

The 'succinct' word family:
        succinct, succinctly, succinctness

Any thoughts about these words?

Exercise. Which is correct?
   a. sucinctly
   b. succincly
   c. succinctly

Write in the vowels

s__cc__nct   s__cc__nctly   s__cc__nctn__ss

Write in the consonants

__u__ __i__ __ __   __u__ __i__ __ __ __ __

__u__ __i__ __ __ __e__ __

Look Say Cover Write Check – do this a few times in the day.

succinct   succinctly

_____   _____

_____   _____

_____   _____

_____   _____

_____   _____

_____   _____

Subsequently

*He **subsequently** decided to give up work.*

---

subsequent + ly = subsequently

sub s**e** qu**e**nt ly   don't forget the e's

Same -*uent*- pattern as *fluent, frequent, eloquent*

Write in the vowels   and the consonants

   s__bs__q__ __ntly   __u__ __e__ue__ __ __ __

My memory tricks, word art, sentences, thoughts.

The 'subsequent' word family:
                        subsequent, subsequently

Any thoughts about these words?

sequ / sec from Latin 'follow, following after': *sequel, sequential, consequence, consecutive, second, sect, subsequent, non sequitur* (= it does not follow)

Exercise. Which is correct?
  a. subsequently
  b. subcequently
  c. subseqently

Write in the vowels

s__bs__q__ __nt   s__bs__q__ __ntly

Write in the consonants

__u__ __e__ue__ __   __u__ __e__ue__ __ __ __

Look Say Cover Write Check – do this a few times in the day.

subsequent   subsequently

_____   _____

_____   _____

_____   _____

_____   _____

_____   _____

_____   _____

Stringently

*Fire regulations are **stringently** enforced here.*

stringent + ly = *stringently*
What words within *stringently* are there?

strin/gent/ly   *The **gent** was strin**gent** about the **string.***
                String the string gently

Any memory tricks?

Write in the vowels   and the consonants

str__ng__ntly   __ __ __ i __ __ e __ __ __ __ __

My memory tricks, word art, sentences, thoughts.

The 'stringent' word family:
                stringent, stringently, stringency
                astringent, astringently, astringency

Any thoughts about these words?

Other -**gent** words: *gent, intelligent, agent, urgent, negligent, belligerent* Write some sentences with these.

Exercise. Which is correct?

   a. stringenly
   b. stringently
   c. stringentley

Write in the vowels

str__ng__nt   str__ng__ntly

str__ng__ncy

Write in the consonants

__ __ __i__ __e__ __   __ __ __i__ __e__ __ __ __

__ __ __i__ __e__ __ __

Look Say Cover Write Check

   stringent   stringently   stringency

_____   _____   _____

_____   _____   _____

_____   _____   _____

_____   _____   _____

_____   _____   _____

_____   _____   _____

Skilfully

*He is a **skilful** and experienced negotiator.*

*In British English we drop the 'l' in *skill* when adding *ful* = *skilful*
skilful + ly = *skilfully*

Write in the vowels   and the consonants

   sk__lf__lly   __ __i__ __u__ __ __

My memory tricks, word art, sentences, thoughts.

Careful: we have *skill* but **skilful**

skilful, skilfully, skilfulness

unskilful, unskilfully, unskilfulness

But we have *skills, skills, skilled, skillet, skill set*

Any thoughts about these words?

*(Careful the American spelling is *skillful* / *skillfully*.)

Exercise. Which is correct?
   a. skilfuly
   b. skilfully
   c. skillfully

Write in the vowels

sk__lf__l   sk__lf__lly

Write in the consonants

__ __i__ __u__   __ __i__ __u__ __ __

Look Say Cover Write Check – do this a few times in the day.

skilful   skilfully

_____   _____

_____   _____

_____   _____

_____   _____

_____   _____

_____   _____

_____   _____

_____   _____

Revision day

Exercise. Which is correct? Use your memory trick &/ or visual
memory.

1. a. sensitivly
   b. sensitively
   c. senstively

2. a. sucinctly
   b. succintly
   c. succinctly

3. a. subsequantly
   b. subsequently
   c. subsquently

4. a. stringantly
   b. sringently
   c. stringently

5. a. skilfully
   b. skillfuly
   c. skillfully

Exercise answers. Which is correct?

1. a. sensitivly
   b. sensitively
   c. senstively

2. a. sucinctly
   b. succintly
   c. succinctly

3. a. subsequantly
   b. subsequently
   c. subsquently

4. a. stringantly
   b. sringently
   c. stringently

5. a. skilfully
   b. skillfuly
   c. skillfully

Notes. Write 3 sentences using these words.

68

Set 1 revision exercise. Which is correct? Can you remember?

1. a. unaceptable
    b. unacceptible
    c. unacceptable

2. a. achievable
    b. acheivable
    c. achieveable

3. a. applicable
    b. aplicable
    c. applyicable

4. a. unprouncable
    b. unpronceable
    c. unpronounceable

5. a. managable
    b. manageable
    c. managerable

Revision day

Exercise answers. Which is correct?

1. ~~a. unaceptable~~
   ~~b. unacceptible~~
   c. unacceptable

2. a. achievable
   ~~b. acheivable~~
   ~~c. achieveable~~

3. a. applicable
   ~~b. aplicable~~
   ~~c. applyicable~~

4. ~~a. unprouncable~~
   ~~b. unpronceable~~
   c. unpronounceable

5. ~~a. managable~~
   b. manageable
   ~~c. managerable~~

Notes

Set 3: Adding -ly (part 2)

appropriately
unfortunately
particularly
significantly
successfully

We have some important words that the test may add -ly to.

appropriate + ly
unfortunate + ly
particular + ly
significant + ly
successful+ ly

Write down the root words and word families for these words?

Appropriately

*She didn't think they were **appropriately** dressed.*

appropriate + ly = *appropriately*
ap/pro/pri/ate/ly

Double p in app! *I'm **appropriately** happy*

*I **ate** <u>appropriate</u>ly and I'm ha<u>pp</u>y.*

Write in the vowels   and the consonants

__ppr__pr__ __t__ly   a__ __ __o__ __a__e__ __

My memory tricks, word art, sentences, thoughts.

The 'appropriate' word family
appropriate, appropriately, appropriateness
appropriacy
inappropriate, inappropriately, inappropriateness

Any thoughts about these words?

Exercise. Which is correct? Use your visual memory &/or memory trick.

    a. apropriately
    b. appropriately
    c. approprietely

Write in the vowels

    __ppr__pr__ __t__   __ppr__pr__ __t__ly

          in__ppr__pr__ __t__

Write in the consonants

        a__ __ __o__ __ia__e

      a__ __ __o__ __ia__e__ __

      i__a__ __ __o__ __ia__e

Look Say Cover Write Check – do this a few times in the day.

appropriate	appropriately	inappropriate
_____	_____	_____
_____	_____	_____
_____	_____	_____
_____	_____	_____
_____	_____	_____
_____	_____	_____

Unfortunately

Unfortunately for Karen, her results weren't good enough

un + fortunate + ly = *unfortunately*

un + fortun + ate + ly

Do you always want to write it with an 'e' like *fortune*?
If so, remember to drop the 'e' when you add 'ate'
*Un<u>fortun</u>ately I **ate** the 'e'!*

Write in the vowels   and the consonants

__nf__rt__n__t__ly   u__ __o__ __u__a__e__ __

My memory tricks, word art, sentences, thoughts.

The 'fortunate' word family:

fortunate, unfortunate
fortunately, unfortunately

Any thoughts about these words?

Exercise. Which is correct? Use your visual memory &/or memory trick.
  a. unfortunately
  b. unfortunetely
  c. unfortuneately

Write in the vowels

f__rt__n__t__   __nf__rt__n__t__

f__rt__n__t__ly   __nf__rt__n__t__ly

Write in the consonants

__o__ __u__a__e   u__ __o__ __u__a__e

__o__ __u__a__e__ __   u__ __o__ __u__a__e__ __

Look Say Cover Write Check – do this a few times in the day.

fortunate   fortunately   unfortunately

_____   _____   _____

_____   _____   _____

_____   _____   _____

_____   _____   _____

_____   _____   _____

_____   _____   _____

Particularly

*I didn't **particularly** want to go, but I did!*

particular + ly = *particularly*

Breaks down into syllables quite well: par / tic / u / lar /ly

par ticu **lar** ly

Difficult bits?

Write in the vowels   and the consonants

p__rt__c__l__rly   __a__ __i__u__a__ __ __

My memory tricks, word art, sentences, thoughts.

The 'particular' word family:
> *particular, particularly, particulars*
> *particularity, particularities*
> *in particular*

Any thoughts about these words?

Exercise. Which is correct?
   a. particulry
   b. paticularly
   c. particularly

Write in the vowels

   p__rt__c__l__r   p__rt__cul__rly

Write in the consonants

   __a__ __i__u__a__   __a__ __i__u__a__ __ __

Look Say Cover Write Check – do this a few times in the day.

   particular   particularly   particulars

   _____   _____   _____

   _____   _____   _____

   _____   _____   _____

   _____   _____   _____

   _____   _____   _____

   _____   _____   _____

   _____   _____   _____

Significantly

*This will help your spelling **significantly**.*

significant + ly = *significantly*

Works well with syllable breakdown:

Notice the i's: **sig nif i** cant ly and **insig**nificantly

Remember the signific**ant,** pleas**ant,** elega**ant ant**

Write in the vowels   and the consonants

s__gn__f__c__ntly   __i__ __i__i__a__ __ __ __

My memory tricks, word art, sentences, thoughts.

The 'significantly' word family
significant, significantly, insignificant, insignificantly

Any thoughts about these words?

Exercise. Which is correct?

  a. significantly
  b. sigificantly
  c. significently

Write in the vowels

    s__gn__f__c__ant   s__gn__f__c__ntly

          __ns__gn__f__c__nt

Write in the consonants

         __i__ __i__i__a__ __

      __i__ __i__i__a__ __ __ __

    i__ __i__ __i__i__a__ __

Look Say Cover Write Check – do this a few times in the day.

  significant   significantly   insignificant

  _____   _____   _____

  _____   _____   _____

  _____   _____   _____

  _____   _____   _____

  _____   _____   _____

Successfully

*Can you complete the test **successfully**?*

success + ful = *successful* + ly = *successfully*
(2 l's when we add -ly)

Think of a mnemonic for the 2 c's and 2 s's

Write in the vowels   and the consonants

   s__cc__ssf__lly   __u__ __e__ __ __ __u__ __ __

My memory tricks, word art, sentences, thoughts.

The 'success' family

success, successes, successful, successfully, successfulness
successes (add **es** to words ending in s, ss, ch, x, z)
success + ful = *successful* + *ly* = *successfully*
unsuccessful, unsuccessfully

Exercise. Which is correct? Use your visual memory &/or memory trick.

   a. succesfuly

   b. successfuly

   c. successfully

Write in the vowels

     s__cc__ssf__l   s__cc__ssf__lly

       __ns__cc__ssf__l

Write in the consonants

__u__ __e__ __ __u__   __u__ __e__ __fu__ __ __

     u__ __u__ __e__ __ __u__

Look Say Cover Write Check – do this a few times in the day.

  successful   successfully   unsuccessful

_____ _____ _____

_____ _____ _____

_____ _____ _____

_____ _____ _____

_____ _____ _____

_____ _____ _____

Revision day

Exercise. Which is correct? Can you remember?

1. a. apropriately
   b. appropriately
   c. approprietely

2. a. unfortunately
   b. unfortunetely
   c. unfortuneately

3. a. particulry
   b. paticularly
   c. particularly

4. a. significantly
   b. sigificantly
   c. significently

5. a. succesfuly
   b. successfuly
   c. successfully

Exercise answers

1. a. appropriately
   b. appropriately
   c. appropriately

2. a. unfortunately
   b. unfortunately
   c. unfortuneately

3. a. particuley
   b. particularly
   c. particularly

4. a. significantly
   b. significantly
   c. significantly

5. a. successfuly
   b. successfully
   c. successfully

-

Notes. Write 3 sentences using these words.

Exercise. Which is correct?

1. a. unaceptable
    b. unacceptible
    c. unacceptable

2. a. achievable
    b. acheivable
    c. achieveable

3. a. applicable
    b. aplicable
    c. applyicable

4. a. unprouncable
    b. unpronceable
    c. unpronounceable

5. a. managable
    b. manageable
    c. managerable

Revision day

Exercise answers

1. a. unacceptable
   b. unacceptible
   c. unacceptable ✓

2. a. achievable ✓
   b. acheivable
   c. achieveable

3. a. applicable ✓
   b. aplicable
   c. applyicable

4. a. unprounceable
   b. unpronceable
   c. unpronounceable ✓

5. a. managable
   b. manageable ✓
   c. managerable

Notes. Write 3 sentences using these words.

Set 2 Revision exercise. Which is correct? Can you remember?

1. a. sensitivly
   b. sensitively
   c. senstively

2. a. sucinctly
   b. succintly
   c. succinctly

3. a. subsequantly
   b. subsequently
   c. subsquently

4. a. stringantly
   b. sringently
   c. stringently

5. a. skilfully
   b. skillfuly
   c. skillfully

Exercise answers

1. a. sensitivly
   b. sensitively
   c. sensitively

2. a. succinctly
   b. succeintly
   c. succinctly

3. a. subsequantly
   b. subsequently
   c. subsquently

4. a. stringantly
   b. stringently
   c. stringently

5. a. skilfully
   b. skillfuly
   c. skillfully

Notes. Write 3 sentences using these words.

Set 4: -ible words

negligible
susceptible
infallible
feasible
responsible

-**ible** words come from Latin. There are <u>no</u> new Latin words!

• The common **-ible** words:
incredible, sensible, possible, responsible, accessible, flexible, legible, collapsible, visible, invisible, edible, reversible, terrible, horrible, impossible, illegible, irresponsible

As a general rule we aren't left with a root word when we take away the **-ible** ending: terr + ible = *terrible*, poss + ible = *possible*

But there are exceptions: *assess/ible, corrupt/ible, destruct/ible, contempt/ible, perfectible, digestible, convertible, exhaustible...*

• Many words ending in 's' or 't' use the **-ible** ending. Notice the **-sible** and **-tible** pattern: *sensible, responsible, visible, collapsible, feasible, possible, accessible, corruptible, susceptible, resistible...*

• Drop the 'e' with **-ible**:
collapse + ible = *collapsible*, response – *responsible, sensible, reducible, defensible, reversible, forcible...*

• Words ending in 'cible' and 'gible' have a soft 'c' and 'g' sound: *forcible, invincible, reducible, submergible, illegible, dirigible, corrigible, negligible...*

• The end 'e' becomes 'y': *horrible – horribly, terrible – terribly, visible – visibly, incredible – incredibly, responsible – responsibly*

Remember, you can add prefixes to some of these words:

visible – invisible	*responsible – irresponsible*
flexible – inflexible	*resistible – irresistible*
edible – inedible	*reversible – irreversible*
accessible – inaccessible	*reducible – irreducible*
feasible – unfeasible	*exhaustible – inexhaustible*
legible – illegible	*possible – impossible*

Negligible

*The difference between the two products is **negligible**.*

---

negligible – neg/li/gible

Notice the 2 g's, 2 e's, 2 i's, 2 l's

Break it down into syllables:

Write in the vowels   and the consonants

   n__gl__g__bl__   __e__ __i__i__ __e

My memory tricks, word art, sentences, thoughts.

The 'negligible' word family
                negligible, negligibly, negligibility

Change the end 'e' to 'y' = *negligibly*

negligible➔ drop the end 'le' and add 'ility' = *negligibility*

Any thoughts about these words?

Other **-gible** words: *eligible, legible, illegible*

Exercise. Which is correct? Use your visual memory &/or memory trick.

a. negliable
b. negligible
c. negligiable

Tick the right one and then cross out the incorrect ones. We don't want to *see* the wrong ones!

Write in the vowels

n__gl__g__bl__   n__gl__g__bly

n__gl__g__ b__l__ty

Write in the consonants

__e__ __i__i__ __e   __e__ __i__i__ __ __

__e__ __i__i__i__ __

Look Say Cover Write Check – do this a few times in the day.

negligible	negligibly	negligibility
_____	_____	_____
_____	_____	_____
_____	_____	_____
_____	_____	_____
_____	_____	_____

Susceptible

*These plants are particularly **susceptible** to frost.*

---

susceptible

Strategies, tricks, syllable breakdown?

Write in the vowels   and the consonants

   s__sc__pt__bl__   __u__ __e__ __i__ __e

My memory tricks, word art, sentences, thoughts.

The 'susceptible' word family

   susceptible, susceptibly, susceptibility, susceptibilities

susceptible ➔ drop the 'le' and add 'ility' = *susceptibility*

susceptibility ➔ change the 'y' to 'ies' = *susceptibilities*

Any thoughts about these words?

Exercise. Which is correct?

    a. suceptibile
    b. susceptible
    c. suceptible

Write in the vowels

    s__sc__pt__ibl__   s__sc__pt__b__l__ty

Write in the consonants

    __u__ __e__ __i__ __e

    __u__ __e__ __i__i__i__ __

Look Say Cover Write Check – do this a few times in the day.

susceptible   susceptibility   susceptibilities

_____   _____   _____

_____   _____   _____

_____   _____   _____

_____   _____   _____

_____   _____   _____

_____   _____   _____

Infallible

*During the rest of the series, Matthews has been **infallible**.*

in + fall + ible = *infallible*   2 i's   **i**nfall**i**ble

Write in the vowels   and the consonants

__nf__ll__bl__   i__ __a__ __i__ __e

My memory tricks, word art, sentences, thoughts.

The 'infallible word family:

infallible, *infallibly, infallibility*
fallible, fallibly, fallibility

Any thoughts about these words?

Exercise. Which is correct?

 a. infalible
 b. infallible
 c. infallable

Write in the vowels

__nf__ll__bl__   __nf__ll__bly

Write in the consonants

i__ __a__ __i__ __e   i__ __a__ __i__ __ __ __

Look Say Cover Write Check – do this a few times in the day.

  infallible   infallibly

  _____   _____

  _____   _____

  _____   _____

  _____   _____

  _____   _____

  _____   _____

Feasible

*The most **feasible** explanation.*

feas + ible = feasible

Write in the vowels   and the consonants

   f__ __s__bl__   __ea__i__ __e

My memory tricks, word art, sentences, thoughts.

The 'feasible' word family:

feasible, feasibly, feasibility
unfeasible, unfeasibly, unfeasibility

Any thoughts about these words?

Exercise. Which is correct?

  a. feasible

  b. feasable

  c. feassible

Write in the vowels

    f__ __s__bl__   __nf__ __s__bl__

        f__ __s__b__l__ty

Write in the consonants

    __ea__i__ __e   u__ __ea__i__ __e

        __ea__i__i__i__ __

Look Say Cover Write Check

  feasible   unfeasible   feasibility

_____   _____   _____

_____   _____   _____

_____   _____   _____

_____   _____   _____

_____   _____   _____

_____   _____   _____

Responsible

*Parents feel **responsible** when things go wrong.*

response ➜ drop the 'e' with ible➜ **responsible**

Strategies?

Write in the vowels   and the consonants

r__sp__ns__bl__   __e__ __o__ __i__ __e

My memory tricks, word art, sentences, thoughts.

The 'responsible' word family
>*responsible, responsibly, responsibility, responsibilities*
>*irresponsible, irresponsibly, irresponsibility*
>*responsibilities* (notice all the i's)

ir + responsible = *irresponsible* (notice the 2 r's)

Which words change the end 'e' to 'y'?

Which words change the 'ly' to 'ility' or 'ilities'?

What are your responsibilities at work, in life?

   a. responsible
   b. responsable
   c. reponsible

Write in the vowels

r__sp__ns__ble   r__sp__ns__bly

r__sp__ns__b__l__ty   r__sp__ns__b__l__t__ __s

__rr__sp__ns__bl__

Write in the consonants

__e__ __o__ __i__ __e   __e__ __o__ __i__ __ __

__e__ __o__ __i__i__ __

__e__ __o__ __i__i__i__ie__

i__ __e__ __on__i__ __e

Look Say Cover Write Check

responsible   irresponsible   responsibilities

_____   _____   _____

_____   _____   _____

_____   _____   _____

_____   _____   _____

Revision day

Exercise. Which is correct?

1. a. neglagible
   b. negligible
   c. neglible

2. a. susceptible
   b. suscepptible
   c. succeptible

3. a. infalible
   b. infallible
   c. infallable

4. a. feesible
   b. feasable
   c. feasible

5. a. responsable
   b. responsibible
   c. responsible

6. a. flexible
   b. flexable

7. a. achievable
   b. acheivable
   c. achieveable

Exercise answers.

1. a. neglagible
   b. negligible
   c. neglible

2. a. susceptible
   b. suscepptible
   c. suceeptible

3. a. infalible
   b. infallible
   c. infallable

4. a. feesible
   b. feasable
   c. feasible

5. a. responsable
   b. responsibible
   c. responsible

6. a. flexible
   b. flexable

7. a. achievable
   b. acheivable
   c. achieveable

Notes

Revision exercise. Which is correct?

1. a. sensitivly
   b. sensitively
   c. senstively

2. a. sucinctly
   b. succintly
   c. succinctly

3. a. subsequantly
   b. subsequently
   c. subsquently

4. a. stringantly
   b. sringently
   c. stringently

5. a. skilfully
   b. skillfuly
   c. skillfully

6. a. infalible
   b. infallible
   c. infallable

7. a. neglagible
   b. negligible
   c. neglible

Exercise answers.

1. ~~a. sensitivly~~
   b. sensitively
   ~~c. senstively~~

2. ~~a. sucinctly~~
   ~~b. succinitly~~
   c. succinctly

3. ~~a. subsequantly~~
   b. subsequently
   ~~c. subsquently~~

4. ~~a. stringantly~~
   ~~b. sringently~~
   c. stringently

5. a. skilfully
   ~~b. skillfuly~~
   ~~c. skillfully~~ (American spelling)

6. ~~a. infalible~~
   b. infallible
   ~~c. infallable~~

7. ~~a. neglagible~~
   b. negligible
   ~~c. neglible~~

Notes

Set 5: Adding prefix 'in' + suffix 'ly'

formal
definite
dependent
conspicuous
competent

Add the prefix **in** and the suffix **ly** to these words:
formal, definite, dependent, conspicuous, competent

prefix **root word** suffix
*in**formal**ly*

Any thoughts?

---

informally
indefinitely
independently
inconspicuously
incompetently

Formal

*She's got a lot of experience but no **formal** qualifications.*

QTS like to test you on **formally** and whether you remember the 2 l's

formal + ly = *formally*
in + formal + ly = *informally*

Write in the vowels   and the consonants

f__rm__lly   __o__ __a__ __ __

My memory tricks, word art, sentences, thoughts.

The 'formal' word family
formal, formally, formality, formalities
formalise/formalize
informal, informally, informality, informalities
formality change the 'y' to 'ies' in the plural – *formalities*

Any thoughts? Write some sentences.

Exercise. Which is correct?
  a. formaly
  b. formelly
  c. formally

Write in the vowels

f__rm__lly   __nf__rm__lly

f__rm__l__ty   __nf__rm__l__t__ __ __

Write in the consonants

__o__ __a__ __y   i__ __o__ __a__ __y

__o__ __a__i__y   i__ __o__ __a__i__ie__

Look Say Cover Write Check – do this a few times in the day.

formally   informally   formalities

_____   _____   _____

_____   _____   _____

_____   _____   _____

_____   _____   _____

_____   _____   _____

Definite

*Are you **definitely** committed to improving your spelling?*

de + finite = definite + ly = **definitely**

de + finite + ly   de /fin/it/e/ly

Can you see **finite** in de**finite**ly?
or Can you see the **it** in *write definitely*?   "*def **in it** ely - **in it**"*

Write in the vowels   and the consonants

  d__f__n__t__ly   __e__i__i__e____

My memory tricks, word art, sentences, thoughts.

The 'definite' word family:
definite, definitely
indefinite, indefinitely, indefiniteness
definition, definitive, definitively

When do we drop the 'e'?

The 'fin' word family comes from Latin for 'end':
*final, finale, finish, infinite, definitive, de**fin**ite*

Exercise. Which is correct?
  a. definately
  b. definitely
  c. definitately

Write in the vowels

d__f__n__t__   d__f__n__t__ly

__nd__f__n__t__

Write in the consonants

__e__i__i__e   __e__i__i__e__ __

i__ __e__i__i__e

Look Say Cover Write Check – do this a few times in the day.

definite	definitely	indefinite
_____	_____	_____
_____	_____	_____
_____	_____	_____
_____	_____	_____
_____	_____	_____

Dependent

*Your pay is **dependent** on your work experience.*

dependent Can you see all those **e**'s? *de pen dent*

in + dependent + ly = **independently**

It's a good one for syllable breakdown!

Write in the vowels	and the consonants
d__p__nd__nt	__e__e____e____

My memory tricks, word art, sentences, thoughts.

Careful: a *dependant* is a child or other relative you give food, money, and a home to: *He still has dependants from a previous marriage.*

The 'dependent' word family:
> *dependent, dependently, dependence, dependency*
> *independent, independence, independents*

Any thoughts about these words?

Exercise. Which is correct?
  a. independence
  b. indpendence
  c. independance

Write in the vowels

d__p__nd__nt

__nd__p__nd__nc__   __nd__p__nd__nt

__nd__p__nd__ntly

Write in the consonants

__e__e__ __e __ __

i__ __e__e__ __e__ __e   i__ __e__e__ __e__ __

i__ __e__e__ __e__ __ __ __

Look Say Cover Write Check – do this a few times in the day.

independent   independence   independently

_____   _____   _____

_____   _____   _____

_____   _____   _____

_____   _____   _____

_____   _____   _____

Conspicuous

*He tried not to look **conspicuous** and moved slowly along the back of the room.*

in + conspicuous = **inconspicuous**
from Latin *inconspicuus* (from *in-* 'not' + *conspicuus* 'clearly visible' + -ous = not clearly visible)

in + conspicuous + ly = **inconspicuously**

Syllable breakdown works well:

Write in the vowels   and the consonants

__nc__nsp__c__ __ __s   i__ __o__ __ __i__uou__

My memory tricks, word art, sentences, thoughts.

The 'conspicuous' word family:
        conspicuous, conspicuously, conspicuousness
        inconspicuous, inconspicuously

Any thoughts about these words?

Other **-uous** words. (The 'u' "you" sound helps you spell these.)
strenuous, continuous, ambiguous, conspicuous, contemptuous, voluptuous, vacuous...

Exercise. Which is correct?
  a. inconspicous
  b. inconspicuous
  c. inconspicuos

Write in the vowels

c__nsp__c__ __ __s   c__nsp__c__ __ __sly

__nc__nsp__c__ __ __s

Write in the consonants

__o__ __ __i__uou__   __o__ __ __i__uou__ __ __

i__ __o__ __ __i__uou__

Look Say Cover Write Check – do this a few times in the day.

conspicuous	conspicuously	inconspicuously
_____	_____	_____
_____	_____	_____
_____	_____	_____
_____	_____	_____
_____	_____	_____
_____	_____	_____
_____	_____	_____

Competent

*He's **competent** at his job, that's all!*

---

competent
Can you see the e's, and the words within words?

We have a **comp** etent, and a com **pet** ent and a compe **tent**
A pet in a tent in a comp!

in + competent = *incompetent* + ly = *incompetently*

Write in the vowels   and the consonants

__nc__mp__t__ntly   i__ __o__ __e__e__ __ __ __ __

My memory tricks, word art, sentences, thoughts.

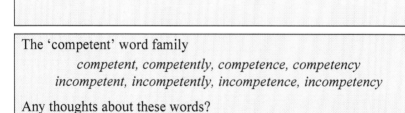

The 'competent' word family
      competent, competently, competence, competency
      incompetent, incompetently, incompetence, incompetency

Any thoughts about these words?

Exercise. Which is correct?
 a. incompetent
 b. incompentent
 c. incomptent

Write in the vowels

c__mp__t__nt   c__mp__t__nc__

__nc__mp__t__nt   __nc__mp__t__nc__

Write in the consonants

__o__ __e__e__ __   __o__ __e__e__ __e

i__ __o__ __e__e__ __   i__ __o__ __e__e__ __e

Look Say Cover Write Check – do this a few times in the day.

competent   competence   incompetence

_____   _____   _____

_____   _____   _____

_____   _____   _____

_____   _____   _____

_____   _____   _____

Revision day

Exercise. Which is correct?

1. a. definately
   b. definitely
   c. definitately

2. a. independantly
   b. independently

3. a. incompetent
   b. incompentent
   c. incomptent

4 a. conspicous
   b. conspicuous
   c. conspicuos

5. a. incompetence
   b. incompetance
   c. incomptence

6. a. formaly
   b. formally

Exercise answers

1. a. definitely
   b. definitely
   c. definitately

2. a. independantly
   b. independently

3. a. incompetent
   b. incompentent
   c. incomptent

4 a. conspicous
   b. conspicuous
   c. conspicuos

5. a. incompetence
   b. incompetence
   c. incomptence

6. a. formaly
   b. formally

Notes. Write 3 sentences with these words.

Set 6: Doubling up rule

omit
admit
prefer
refer
expel

When we add some vowel suffixes to these words we double up the last consonant, why? Can you remember the exceptions?

(Go to page 35 to refresh your memory on the 1:1:1 doubling up rule.)

Add   **-ing, -ed, -ence** or **-ance** to these words

omit – _____

admit – _____

prefer – _____

refer – _____

expel – _____

Answers and explanation

The 1:1:1 doubling up rule is also used for longer words when the **second** syllable is stressed. And this is where QTS like to test you, so learn these words and the exceptions using memory tricks or rhymes.

omit – *omitting, omitted*

admit – *admitting, admittance, admitted*

prefer – *preferred, preferring*
(Not *preference, preferable, preferential, preferentially*)

refer – referred, referring
(Not *ref**erence, referendum, referencing*)

expel – *expelled, expelling, expellable, expellee, expeller*
(expels – remember to only double up with vowel suffixes)

Other words worth learning:

be**gin** – *begi**nn**er, beginning*

forget – *forge**tt**ing, forgettable, unforgettable*

forgot – *forgotten*

regret – *regrettable, regretting, regretted*

forbid – *forbidden, forbidding*

submit – *submitting, submitted*

equip – *equipped, equipping* (*NOT* equipment - why?)

defer – *deferred, deferring, deferral* (NOT *def**erence, deferential, deferment*)

transfer – *transferring, transferred* (NOT ***trans**ference, transferable*)

occur – *occurring, occurred, occurrence*

concur – *concurring, concurred*

transfer – *transferring, transferred* (NOT ***trans**ference, transferable*)

deter – *deterring, deterrent, deterrence*

Write some sentences, tricks, thoughts, missing vowels and consonants, and do the Look Say Cover Write method...

omit – *omitting, omitted*

admit – *admitting, admittance, admitted*

prefer – *preferred, preferring*
(Not *preference, preferable, preferential, preferentially)*

refer – referred, referring
(Not **ref***erence, referendum, referencing*)

expel – *expelled, expelling, expellable, expellee, expeller*

occur – *occurring, occurred, occurrence*

transfer – *transferring, transferred*
(NOT **trans***ference, transferable*)

deter – *deterring, deterrent, deterrence*

Revision Which is correct?

1. a. deterrent
   b. deterrant
   c. deterent

2. a. expeled
   b. expelled

3. a. preference
   b. preferrence
   c. preferance

4. a. transfered
   b. transferred

5. a. ocurrence
   b. occurrence
   c. occurrance

6. a. deterence
   b. detterence
   c. deterrence

7. a. admittence
   b. admitence
   c. admittance

8. a. preferable
   b. preferrable
   c. prefferable

9. a. omitted
   b. ommited
   c. ommitted

10. a. regretable
    b. regrettible
    c. regrettable

Revision Answers

1. a. deterrent
   b. deterrant
   c. deterent

2. a. expeled
   b. expelled

3. a. preference
   b. preferrence
   c. preferance

4. a. transfered
   b. transferred

5. a. occurence
   b. occurrence
   c. occurrance

6. a. deterence
   b. detterence
   c. deterrence

7. a. admittence
   b. admitence
   c. admittance

8. a. preferable
   b. preferrable
   c. prefferable

9. a. omitted
   b. ommited
   c. ommitted

10. a. regretable
    b. regrettible
    c. regrettable

Revision

Exercise. Which is correct? Can you remember?

1. a. unfortunately
   b. unfortunetely

2. a. sucinctly
   b. succintly
   c. succinctly

3. a. subsequantly
   b. subsequently

4. a. stringantly
   b. stringently

5. a. skilfully
   b. skillfuly
   c. skillfully

6. a. definately
   b. definitely

7. a. independently
   b. independantly

8. a. sucessfuly
   b. successfuly
   c. successfully

Exercise answers

1. a. unfortunately

2. c. succinctly

3. b. subsequently

4. b. stringently

5. a. skilfully

6. b. definitely

7. a. independently

8. c. successfully

Notes

Revision day

Write in the 3-letter endings

1. defin_____

2. signific_____

3. success_____

4 independ_____

5. incompet_____

6. unfortun_____

7. string_____

8. succi_____

9. inappropri_____

Exercise answers

1. defin<u>ite</u>
2. signific<u>ant</u>
3. success<u>ful</u>
4. independ<u>ent</u>
5. incompet<u>ent</u>
6. unfortun<u>ate</u>
7. string<u>ent</u>
8. succi<u>nct</u>
9. inappropri<u>ate</u>

Notes

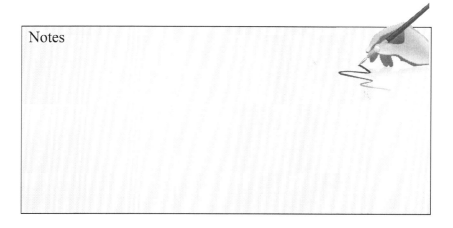

127

Revision day

Add the **-able** or **-ible** endings

1. neglig_____

2. respons_____

3. manage_____

4. feas_____

5. unpronounce_____

6. suscept_____

7. infall_____

8. achiev_____

9. prefer_____

10. suscept_____

Exercise answers

Add the **-able** or **-ible** endings

1. negligible

2. responsible

3. manageable

4. feasible

5. unpronounceable

6. susceptible

7. infallible

8. achievable

9. preferable

10. susceptible

Notes

Exercise
Write in the 2 missing vowels

1. ach__ __vable

2. unpron__ __nceable

3. f__ __sible

4. indef__n__te

5. unfortun__t__ly

6. appropr__ __tely

7. inconspic__ __us

8. negl__g__ble

9. manag__ __ble

10. subs__qu__ntly

11. incomp__t__nce

Exercise answers

1. achievable

2. unpronounceable

3. feasible

4. indefinite

5. unfortunately

6. appropriately

7. inconspicuous

8. negligible

9. manageable

10. subsequently

11. incompetence

Notes

Exercise

Look at these words we've studied, say them, cover them and write them in the right gaps below:

inconspicuous
inapplicable
infallible
incompetence
informally

1. Please dress _____

2. Computers aren't _____ so back up your work.

3. These regulations are _____ to visitors from outside the European Union.

4. Their _____ is astounding.

5. They work in an _____ red-brick building.

Exercise Answers

1. Please dress <u>informally.</u>

2. Computers aren't <u>infallible</u> so back up your work.

3. These regulations are <u>inapplicable</u> to visitors from outside the European Union.

4. Their <u>incompetence</u> is astounding.

5. They work in an <u>inconspicuous</u> red-brick building.

Notes

Set 7: 'x' words

exaggerated
exhaustive
existence
anxious
anxiety

Write the word families for these words. Start with the root word and add, if possible, prefixes, suffixes, suffixes for grammar, plurals, etc. Then check and compare over the next few pages.

Exaggerated

*She **exaggerated** the whole event to make it sound interesting.*

The 'ex' sounds like "eggs!" Can you see the 2 g's in *eggs*? Use this to remember that there are two g's in *exaggerated, exaggerate, exaggerating, exaggeration*, etc.

A memory trick could be: "I **ate** two **ex**tra **eggs**" = **ex**agg**e**rated

Write in the vowels   and the consonants

__x__gg__r__t__d   e__a__ __e__a__e__

My memory tricks, word art, sentences, thoughts.

The 'exaggerate' word family:
*exaggerate, exaggerates, exaggerated, exaggeratedly,
exaggerating, exaggeration*

Any thoughts about these words? Which words drop the 'e'?

Exercise. Which is correct?
  a. exagerated
  b. exaggerated
  c. exaggerrated

Write in the vowels

    __x__gg__r__t__   __x__gg__r__t__d

    __x__gg__r__t__ng   __x__gg__r__t__ __n

Write in the consonants

    e__a__ __e__a__e   e__a__ __e__a__e__

    e__a__ __e__a__i__ __   e__a__ __e__a__io__

Look Say Cover (see, think, memory trick) Write Check

exaggerated   exaggerating   exaggeration

_____   _____   _____

_____   _____   _____

_____   _____   _____

_____   _____   _____

_____   _____   _____

_____   _____   _____

Exhaustive

*An **exhaustive** study.*

> *exhaustive*   ex haust ive
>
> We have the tricky -au- pattern.
> *always **understanding** is exha**u**sting*

Write in the vowels   and the consonants

__xh__ __st__v__   e__ __au__ __i__e

My memory tricks, word art, sentences, thoughts.

The 'exhaust' word family:

> *exhaust, exhausts, exhausted*
> *exhaustive, exhaustively, exhaustiveness, inexhaustible*
> *exhaustion*

Any thoughts about these words?

Exercise. Which is correct?
  a. exhaustive
  b. exahaustive
  c. exhuastive

Write in the vowels

__xh__ __st__v__   __xh__ __st__v__ly

__n__xh__ __st__bl__

Write in the consonants

e__ __au__ __i__e   e__ __au__ __i__e__ __

i__e__ __au__ __i__ __e

Look Say Cover (see, think, memory trick) Write Check

exhaustive   exhaustively   inexhaustible

_____   _____   _____

_____   _____   _____

_____   _____   _____

_____   _____   _____

_____   _____   _____

_____   _____   _____

Existence

*Television has become part of our everyday **existence**.*

existence   Notice the e's   **e**x is t**e**nc**e**

Careful: *tence* with a 'c' ➜ ex is t**ence**
*My exist**ence** is ruled by **pence***

existent ➜ existence

Write in the vowels   and the consonants

__x__st__nc__   e__i____e____e

My memory tricks, word art, sentences, thoughts.

The 'exist' word family:

exist, exists, existed
existent, existence
non-existent, non-existence
existential, existentialism

Any thoughts about these words?

Exercise. Which is correct?
  a. existense
  b. existence
  c. existance

Write in the vowels

__x__st__nt   __x__st__nc__

n__n-__x__st__nt

Write in the consonants

e__i__ __e__ __   e__i__ __e__ __e

__o__-e__i__ __e__ __

Look Say Cover (see, think, memory trick) Write Check
  existent   existence   non-existent

  _____   _____   _____

  _____   _____   _____

  _____   _____   _____

  _____   _____   _____

  _____   _____   _____

  _____   _____   _____

Anxious anxiety

*His **anxiety** made everyone **anxious**.*

The QTS site says, "You have to learn [anxiety] by heart."
But you can learn it with the others in the **anxi-** pattern.

anxious ➜ 2 syllables   an /xious
'xious' = "*shus*" also *noxious, obnoxious*

anxiety ➜ 4 syllables   an /xi /e /ty   *an extra var**iety** of anx**iety***

Memory tricks?

Write in the vowels   and the consonants

__nx__ __ __s   a__ __iou__

__nx__ __ty   a__ __ie__ __

My memory tricks, word art, sentences, thoughts.

The 'anxi..." word family:
         anxious, anxiously, anxiousness, overanxious
         anxiety, anxieties, overanxiety

Any thoughts about these words? Write some sentences.

Exercise. Which is correct?
 a. anxous   a. anxiety
 b. anxious   b. anxiaty
 c. anxiouos   c. ansxiety

Write in the vowels

   __nx__ __ __s __nx__ __ty

  __nx__ __ __sly __nx__ __t__ __s

Write in the consonants

   a__ __iou__ a__ __ie__ __

  a__ __iou__ __ __ a__ __ie__ie__

Look Say Cover (see, think, memory trick) Write Check

anxious   anxiously   anxiousness

_____ _____ _____

_____ _____ _____

_____ _____ _____

anxiety   anxieties

_____ _____

_____ _____

_____ _____

Exercise. Write in 'x' words

1. What's another word for 'to be worried' – to be _____

2. What's the plural of anxiety – _____

3. What's the word that means to describe something in a way that makes it seem better, worse, larger, more important than it really is to _____

4. What's the words for the state of being a real or living thing, or of being present in a particular place, time, or situation – to be in _____

5. Thorough, complete, including all possibilities, very thorough

   – _____

Which is correct?

1. a. anxous
   b. anxious
   c. anxiouos

2. a. anxiety
   b. anxiaty
   c. ansxiety

Set 7   Exercise Answers

1. What's another word for 'to be worried' – to be <u>anxious</u>

2. What's the plural of anxiety – <u>anxieties</u>

3. What's the word that means to describe something in a way that makes it seem better, worse, larger, more important than it really is – to <u>exaggerate</u>

4. What's the word for the state of being a real or living thing, or of being present in a particular place, time, or situation – to be in <u>existence</u>

5. Thorough, complete, including all possibilities, very thorough – <u>exhaustive</u>

Answers
1. a. anxous
   b. anxious
   c. anxiouos

2. a. anxiety
   b. anxiaty
   c. ansxiety

Notes

Set 8: 'y' to 'i' rule

justify
defy
apply
ready
compulsory

If a word ends in a **consonant** + *y*, then 'y' changes to 'i' (but not with 'i' suffixes *-ing, -ish /ible* – too many i's otherwise)

beau**ty** – beauti + ful = *beautiful, beautify, beautician*
hap**py** – *happiness, happily, happier, happiest*
ang**ry** – *angrier, angriest, angrily*
bu**sy** – *busier, busiest, busily, business*
      (We also use *busyness* – a noun – *The busyness of life.)*

apply – *applied, application, applicable* (not *applying*)
justify – *justified, justifiable (*but *justifying)*
ready – *readily, readiness, readier, readiest*
defy – *defied, defiant, defiance*
compulsory – *compulsorily, compulsoriness*

To make plurals and third person verbs change the **y** to **ies**
defy – *defies*
apply – *applies*
justify – *justifies*

Justify

*He thinks he was **justified** in taking the money.*

The 'justify' word family

Change the 'y' to 'ies' ➔*justifies*   See the 2 i's **justifies**

Change the 'y' to 'i' + ed' ➔*justified*

Change the 'y' to 'iable' ➔*justifiable*

Change the 'y' to 'iably' ➔*justifiably*

Change the 'y' to 'ication' ➔*justification*

But leave the 'y' + 'ing' ➔*justifying*

They break into syllables:

Write in the vowels   and the consonants

j__st__f__ __s   __u__ __i__ie__

j__st__f__ __bl__   __u__ __i__ia__ __e

j__st__f__ __bly   __u__ __i__ia__ __ __

My memory tricks, word art, sentences, thoughts.

146

Exercise. Which is correct?
   a. justifable
   b. justifyable
   c. justifiable

Other words in the 'justify' family

unjustified unjustifiable unjustifiably
justifiability, justifiableness
justificatory, justificative
justifier

Thoughts?

Look Say Cover (see, think, memory trick) Write Check
   justify   justified   justifiably

_____   _____   _____

_____   _____   _____

_____   _____   _____

_____   _____   _____

_____   _____   _____

_____   _____   _____

Defy

*Their actions **defy** explanation.*

The 'defy' word family

Change the 'y' to 'ies' ➔*defies*

Change the 'y' to 'i' + 'ed' ➔*defied*

But leave the 'y' + 'ing' ➔*defying*

Write in the vowels	and the consonants
d__f__ __s	__e__ie__
d__f__ __d	__e__ie__
d__fy__ng	__e__ __i__ __

My memory tricks, word art, sentences, thoughts.

148

Exercise. Which is correct?
   a. defyed
   b. defied

Notes

Look Say Cover (see, think, memory trick) Write Check
   defy   defies   defying

   _____   _____   _____

   _____   _____   _____

   _____   _____   _____

   _____   _____   _____

Apply

*To **apply** for the job, fill in an **application**.*

apply spelling rules

Change the 'y' to 'ies' ➔ *applies*

Change the 'y' to 'i' + ed' ➔ *applied*

Change the 'y' to 'icable' ➔ *applicable*   app<u>l</u>ic<u>a</u>ble

Change the 'y' to 'ication' ➔ *application*

But leave the 'y' + 'ing' ➔ *applying*

Don't forget the 2 p's: *An **app** is a computer **app**lication*

Use this along with syllable breakdown, sound and visual memory to help with *ap pli ca tion* and *ap pli ca ble*

Write in the vowels   and the consonants

__ppl__ __s   a__ __ __ie__

__ppl__ __d   a__ __ __ie__

__ppl__c__t__ __n   a__ __ __i__a__io__

__ppl__c__bl__   a__ __ __i__a__ __e

My memory tricks, word art, sentences, thoughts.

Exercise. Which is correct?
   a. applycable
   b. applicible
   c. applicable

'apply' word family:

> apply, applies, applied, applying, applier
> applicant, applicants
> applicator, applicatory
> applicable, applicably, applicability, applicableness
> appliance
> applicative

Thoughts?

Look Say Cover (see, think, memory trick) Write Check

application	applicable	applied
_____	_____	_____
_____	_____	_____
_____	_____	_____
_____	_____	_____
_____	_____	_____
_____	_____	_____

Ready

The 'ready word family

Change the 'y' to 'i' + ly' ➜ *readily*

Change the 'y' to 'i' + ness ➜ *readiness*

Change the 'y' to 'i' + 'er' ➜ *readier*

Change the 'y' to 'i' + 'est' ➜ *readiest*

Break into syllables:

Write in the vowels   and the consonants

    r__ __d__ly   __ea__i__ __

    r__ __d_n__ss   __ea__i__e__ __

My memory tricks, word art, sentences, thoughts.

Exercise. Which is correct?
   a. readiness
   b. readyness

Look Say Cover (see, think, memory trick) Write Check
                readily   readiness

   _____   _____

   _____   _____

   _____   _____

   _____   _____

   _____   _____

   _____   _____

   _____   _____

   _____   _____

Compulsory

Compulsory education

The 'compulsory' word family

Change the 'y' to 'i' + 'ly' ➔ *compulsorily*

Change the 'y' to 'i' + 'ness' ➔ *compulsoriness*

compulsory (A key teaching word! The QTS are testing your knowledge of letter patterns and visual memory – is it *-ery, -ory* or *-ary*?)

You could use syllable breakdown com /pul /so / ry – say it slow and exaggerated and visualise it.

Or come up with a memory trick: *sorry it's compulsory*

Write in the vowels   and the consonants

    c__mp__ls__ry   __o__ __u__ __o__ __

    c__mp__ls__r__ly   __o__ __u__ __o__i__ __

My memory tricks, word art, sentences, thoughts.

154

Exercise. Which is correct?
- a. compulsery
- b. compulsory
- c. compulsary

Notes?

Look Say Cover (see, think, memory trick) Write Check

compulsory   compulsorily

_____   _____

_____   _____

_____   _____

_____   _____

Revision day

Which is correct?

1. a. justifable
   b. justifyable
   c. justifiable

2. a. defyed
   b. defied

3. a. applycable
   b. applicible
   c. applicable

4. a. readiness
   b. readyness

5. a. compulsery
   b. compulsory
   c. compulsary

Exercise Answers

1. a. justifable
   b. justifyable
   c. justifiable

2. a. defyed
   b. defied

3. a. applyeable
   b. applieible
   c. applicable

4. a. readiness
   b. readyness

5. a. compulsery
   b. compulsory
   c. compulsary

Notes

Revision exercise

1. a. negligible
   b. negliable
   c. neglibible

2. a. approprietely
   b. apropriately
   c. appropriately

3. a. stringently
   b. stringantly
   c. strigently

4. a. achievable
   b. acheivable
   c. achieveable

5. a. unfortunatly
   b. unfortunately
   c. unfortuneatetly

6. a. sucinctly
   b. succincly
   c. succinctly

7. a. inconspicous
   b. inconspicuos
   c. inconspicuous

8. a. preferance
   b. preference
   c. preferrence

Revision exercise

1. a. negligible
   b. negliable
   c. neglibible

2. a. approprietely
   b. appropriately
   c. appropriately

3. a. stringently
   b. stringantly
   c. strigently

4. a. achievable
   b. acheivable
   c. achieveable

5. a. unfortunatly
   b. unfortunately
   c. unfortuneatetly

6. a. sucinetly
   b. succinely
   c. succinctly

7. a. inconspicous
   b. inconspicuos
   c. inconspicuous

8. a. preference
   b. preference
   c. preferrence

Set 9: Tricky letters

stationary or stationery
bureaucratic
entrepreneur
curriculum
acquaintance

Which ones do you find hard to spell?

Read them, cover them and see if you can spell them.

Which letters do you find tricky?

Stationary or stationery

stationery or stationary?

stationery has envelopes, pens, paper, etc.
A *stationer* is someone who sells paper, pens, etc.

stationary = stop at the station

Notes

Bureaucratic

*The company was inefficient because it was highly **bureaucratic**.*

Fill in the vowels   and consonants

b__r__ __ __cr__t__c   __u__eau__ __a__i__

My memory tricks, word art, sentences, thoughts.

Word family

bureaucrat, bureaucratic, bureaucratically
bureaucracy

Fill in the vowels

b__r__ __ __cr__t   b__r__ __ __cr__t__c

b__r__ __ __cr__cy

Exercise. Which is correct?

a. bureacratic
b. bureaucratic
c. buroeucratic

Look Say Cover Write Check

bureaucrat   **bureaucratic**   **bureaucracy**

_____   _____   _____

_____   _____   _____

_____   _____   _____

_____   _____   _____

_____   _____   _____

_____   _____   _____

_____   _____   _____

Entrepreneur

*She'll make money – she's got that **entrepreneurial** spirit.*

---

entrepreneur

See all the e's **entrepreneur**

Syllable breakdown?

Write in the vowels   and the consonants

__ntr__pr__n__ __r   e__ __ __e__ __e__eu__

My memory tricks, word art, sentences, thoughts.

The 'entrepreneur' word family:

*entrepreneur, entrepreneurs,
entrepreneurial, entrepreneurialism,
entrepreneurship*

Exercise. Which is correct?
a. entrepreneaur
b. entrpreneur
c. entrepreneur

Fill in the vowels

__ntr__pr__n__ __r

__ntr__pr__n__ __r__ __l

Fill in the consonants

e__ __ __e__ __e__eu__

e__ __ __e__ __e__eu__ia__

Look Say Cover Write Check

entrepreneur   entrepreneurial

_____   _____

_____   _____

_____   _____

_____   _____

_____   _____

_____   _____

Curriculum

*The national **curriculum.***

curriculum See all the u's and 2 r's **curriculum**

Syllable breakdown, memory tricks?

Write in the vowels

c__rr__c__l__m

and the consonants

__u__ __i__u__u__

My memory tricks, word art, sentences, thoughts.

The 'curricular' word family:

curriculum, curriculum vitae
curricular, cross-curricular, extracurricular
plural: *curricula or curriculums*

Exercise. Which is correct?

a. curiculum

b. curriculum

c. curricculum

Fill in the vowels

c__rr__c__l__m   __xtr__c__rr__c__l__r

Fill in the consonants

__u__ __i__u__u__

e__ __ __a__u__ __i__u__a__

Look Say Cover Write Check

    curriculum   extracurricular

_____   _____

_____   _____

_____   _____

_____   _____

_____   _____

Acquaintance

*He gradually lost contact with all his old **acquaintances**.*

acquaintance / acquaintances
See all the a's **acquaintance**

acquaint – acquainted – acquaintance – acquaintances

Syllable breakdown, memory tricks, words within words?

Fill in the vowels   and the consonants

__cq__ __ __nt__nc__   a__ __uai__ __a__ __e

My memory tricks, word art, sentences, thoughts.

Exercise. Which is correct?
a. acquaintance
b. acquaintence
c. acquainttance

Fill in the vowels

__cq__ __ __nt__nc__   __cq__ __ __nt__nc__s

Fill in the consonants

a__ __uai__ __a__ __e   a__ __uai__ __a__ __e__

Look Say Cover Write Check

acquaintance   acquaintances

_____   _____

_____   _____

_____   _____

_____   _____

_____   _____

_____   _____

Revision

Exercise.

Which is correct?

1. a. The train was stationery for 20 minutes
   b. The train was stationary for 20 minutes

2. a. bureacratic
   b. bureaucratic
   c. buroeucratic

3. a. entrepreneaur
   b. entrpreneur
   c. entrepreneur

4. a. curiculum
   b. curriculum
   c. curricculum

5. a. acquaintance
   b. acquaintence
   c. acquainttance

Exercise Answers.

1. a. The train was stationery for 20 minutes
   b. The train was stationary for 20 minutes

2. a. bureacratic
   b. bureaucratic
   c. buroeucratic

3. a. entrepreneaur
   b. entrpreneur
   c. entrepreneur

4. a. curiculum
   b. curriculum
   c. curriceulum

5. a. acquaintance
   b. acquaintence
   c. acquainttance

Revision day

Which is correct? Remember to use your knowledge of patterns, rules, your memory tricks, syllable breakdown or visual memory to help.

1. a. manageable
   b. managable

2. a. sensitively
   b. sensitivly

3. a. significantly
   b. significently

4. a. exagerated
   b. exagerrated
   c. exaggerated

5. a. incompetance
   b. incompetence

6. a. compulsory
   b. compulsery
   c. compulsury

7. a. infallible
   b. infallable

8. a. existence
   b. existance

9. a. formaly
   b. formally

Answers

Did you use your knowledge of patterns, rules, your memory tricks or visual memory to help?

1. a. manageable
   b. managable

2. a. sensitively
   b. sensitivly

3. a. significantly
   b. significently

4. a. exagerated
   b. exagerrated
   c. exaggerated

5. a. incompetance
   b. incompetence

6. a. compulsory
   b. compulsery
   c. compulsury

7. a. infallible
   b. infallable

8. a. existence
   b. existance

9. a. formaly
   b. formally

Revision exercise

Write in the **ible** or **able** endings

1. infall_____

2. manage_____

3. respons_____

4. achiev_____

5. justifi_____

6. feas_____

7. prefer_____

8. applic_____

Answers

Write in the **ible** or **able** endings

1. infallible

2. manageable

3. responsible

4. achievable

5. justifiable

6. feasible

7. preferable

8. applicable

Notes

Set 10: Drop the 'i' rule

Some words ending in **-ain**, **-aim**, **-ail** drop the 'i' when adding certain vowel endings. Also, the long vowel sound becomes a sound short, which helps pronunciation and spelling.

> expl**ain** – expl**an**ation, explanatory, self-explanatory
> Spain – Spaniard, Spanish
> procl**aim** – procl**am**ation
> reclaim – reclamation
> acclaim – acclamation
> prev**ail** – prev**al**ent, prevalence

We also change the **-ai-** to **-e-** in:

> maint**ain** – maint**en**ance (but maintainable)
> detain – detention
> retain – retention
> attain – attention
> sustain – sustenance
> abstain – abstention

Notice the long vowel sound becomes a sound short, which helps pronunciation and spelling!

Notes

Fill in the vowels

__xpl__ __n   expl__n__t__ __n   expl__n__t__ry

pr__cl__ __m   pr__cl__m__t__ __n

m__ __nt__ __n   m__ __nt__n__nc__

pr__v__ __l   pr__v__l__nt   pr__v__l__nc__

Fill in the consonants

e__ __ __ai__   e__ __ __ __a__a__io__

e__ __ __ __a__a__o__ __

__ __o__ __ai__   __ __o__ __a__a__io__

__ai__ __ai__   __ai __ __e__a__ __e

__ __e__ai__   __ __e__a__e__ __

__ __e__a__e__ __e

If you find any of these words difficult use the Look Say Cover
Write Check method

Notes

Exercise

Which is correct?

1. a. maintenance
   b. maintainence
   c. maintenence

2. a. explanation
   b. explaination
   c. explainaition

3. a. explainatory
   b. explainatery
   c. explanatory

4. a. maintenable
   b. maintainable
   c. mainatainible

5. a. prevailant
   b. prevalent
   c. prevalant

6. a. proclaimation
   b. proclamaition
   c. proclamation

Exercise Answers

Which is correct?

1. a maintenance
    b. maintainence
    c. maintenence

2. a. explanation
    b. explaination
    c. explainaition

3. a. explainatory
    b. explainatery
    c. explanatory

4. a. maintenable
    b. maintainable
    c. mainatainible

5. a. prevailant
    b. prevalent
    c. prevalant

6. a. proclaimation
    b. proclamaition
    c. proclamation

Revision

Write in the 3-letter endings

1. compuls_____

2. signific_____

3. inconspicu_____

4. skil_____

5. appropri_____

6. exagger_____

7. unfortun_____

8. success_____

9. independ_____

10. indefin_____

Answers

Write in the 3-letter endings

1. compulsory

2. significant

3. inconspicuous

4. skilful

5. appropriate

6. exaggerate

7. unfortunate

8. successful

9. independent

10. indefinite

Set 11: -ous pattern and rules

conscientious
courteous
meticulous
synonymous

-ous is from Latin meaning 'full of' or 'like': *glorious* = full of glory, *joyous* = full of joy, *courageous* = full of courage.

1. -ous is usually added to root words. (Some root words have disappeared over time, or only a portion of the word remains.)
    danger + ous = *dangerous*, hazard + ous = *hazardous*
    marvel + ous = *marvellous* (+ double 'l' rule)
    joyous, poisonous, cancerous, perilous, murderous…
    fabulous, numerous, horrendous, anonymous…

2. When we add **-ous** to words ending in **-our,** we drop the '**u**'
    humour – humorous, glamour – glamorous,
    labour – laborious, odour – odorous
    vigour – vigorous, rigour – rigorous

3. We drop the 'e' when adding **-ous**
    fame + ous = famous   *nerve + ous = nervous*
    adventure – adventurous   *ridicule – ridiculous,*
    blaspheme – blasphemous   *torture – torturous…*

4. -geous Keep the 'e' to keep the soft "g" sound.
    outrage – outrageous, courageous, advantageous, gorgeous.

5. These two words ending in **-f** change to **-vous**
    grief – grievous, mischief – mischievous

6. Just add **-ly:**
    anxious + ly = *anxiously, seriously, enormously, famously,*
    dangerously, curiously, mysteriously, nervously, courageously…

7. y to i + ous = **-ious** (the pronunciation helps)
    glory – glorious, furious, various, envious, luxurious,
    harmonious, studious.
Also: *serious, curious, notorious, previous, bilious*
"shus" sound in *vicious, conscious, precious, delicious, gracious…*

Conscientious

*A **conscientious** student.*

conscientious

Memory tricks?

Write in the vowels   and the consonants

c__nsc__ __nt__ __ __s   __o__ __ __ie__ __iou__

My memory tricks, word art, sentences, thoughts.

Word family:
conscientious, conscientiously, conscientiousness

Any thoughts about these words?

The 'sci' word family from the Latin 'to know'
science, conscience, conscious, omniscience, subconscious,
conscientious

Exercise. Which is correct?
  a. conscientious
  b. conciențious
  c. conscientous

Write in the vowels

c__nsc__ __nt__ __ __s   c__nsc__ __nt__ __ __sly

Write in the consonants

__o__ __ __ie__ __iou__

__o__ __ __ __ie__ __iou__ __ __

Look Say Cover (see, think, memory trick) Write Check

         conscientious   conscientiously

    _____   _____

    _____   _____

    _____   _____

    _____   _____

    _____   _____

Courteous

*He was a very **courteous** man with huge respect for everyone.*

courteous

Memory tricks, words within the word, syllable breakdown?

Write in the vowels   and the consonants

c__ __rt__ __ __s   __ou__ __eou__

My memory tricks, word art, sentences, thoughts.

Word family:

            courteous, courteously, courteousness

Any thoughts about these words?

Words with the same **-eous** pattern.
Pronunciation and syllable breakdown help with these.
miscellaneous, nauseous, hideous, spontaneous
gorgeous, courageous, advantageous, outrageous

Exercise. Which is correct?
- a. courtous
- b. couteous
- c. courteous

Write in the vowels

c__ __rt__ __ __s   c__ __rt__ __ __sly

Write in the consonants

__ou__ __eou__   __ou__ __eou__ __ __ __

Look Say Cover (see, think, memory trick) Write Check

courteous   courteously

_____   _____

_____   _____

_____   _____

_____   _____

_____   _____

_____   _____

_____   _____

Meticulous

The film is visually spectacular, with epic battle scenes and **meticulous** *attention to period detail.*

---

meticulous

Rhymes with rid**iculous**
Is it rid<u>iculous</u> to be met<u>iculous</u>?

Memory tricks, syllable breakdown?

Write in the vowels   and the consonants

m__t__c__l____s   __e__i__u__ou__

My memory tricks, word art, sentences, thoughts.

Word family:
meticulous, meticulously, meticulousness

Any thoughts about these words?

Other **-lous** words: *jealous, marvellous, perilous*
-ulous words: *fabulous, ridiculous*

Exercise. Which is correct?
 a. meticlous
 b. meticulous
 c. metickulous

Write in the vowels

 m__t__c__l____s   m__t__c__l____sly

Write in the consonants

 __e__i__u__ou__   __e__i__u__ou__ __ __

Look Say Cover (see, think, memory trick) Write Check
        meticulous   meticulously

        _____   _____

        _____   _____

        _____   _____

        _____   _____

        _____   _____

Synonymous

The words "annoyed" and "irritated" are more or less ***synonymous***.

---

synonymous

Similar patterns in *anonymous, eponymous*

Memory tricks, syllable breakdown, word within the word?

Write in the vowels   and the consonants

   syn__nym__ __s   __ __ __o__ __ __ou__

My memory tricks, word art, sentences, thoughts.

Word family:

synonym, synonyms,
synonymous, synonymously, synonymousness

Any thoughts about these words?

Exercise. Which is correct?
- a. synoymous
- b. synonymous
- c. synonynmous

Write in the vowels

syn__nym   syn__nym__ __s   syn__nym__ __sly

Write in the consonants

__ __ __o__ __ __   __ __ __o__ __ __ou__

__ __ __o__ __ __ou__ __ __

Look Say Cover Write Check

synonym	synonymous	synonymously

Exercise. Which is correct?

1. a. conscientious
   b. concientious
   c. conscientous

2. a. courtous
   b. couteous
   c. courteous

3. a. meticlous
   b. meticulous
   c. metickulous

4. a. synoymous
   b. synonymous
   c. synonynmous

5. a. anxous
   b. anxious
   c. anixious

6. a. inconspicuous
   b. inconspicous
   c. inconpicuous

Exercise Answers

1. a. conscientious
   b. concientious
   c. conscientous

2. a. courtous
   b. couteous
   c. courteous

3. a. meticlous
   b. meticulous
   c. metickulous

4. a. synoymous
   b. synonymous
   c. synonynmous

5. a. anxous
   b. anxious
   c. anixious

6. a. inconspicuous
   b. inconspicous
   c. inconpicuous

Write 3 sentences with these -ous words

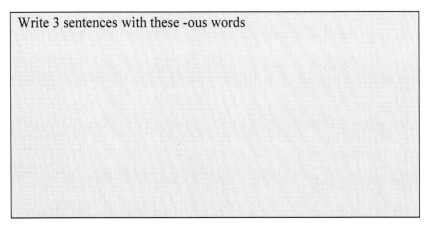

Exercise. Can you think of other **-ous** words that go below?

1. When something tastes yummy – it's _____

2. When someone is well known and everyone knows them they're _____

3. When you're very careful you're _____

4. When there are a large <u>number</u> of things - _____

5. Another word for beautiful is _____

6. My office is very big and roomy it's _____

7. Another word for very, very big _____

8. Another word for worried, nervous _____

-ous Exercise Answers

Write in the **-ous** words

1. When something tastes yummy – it's <u>delicious</u>

2. When someone is well known, everyone knows
   them – <u>famous</u>

3. When you're very careful you're – <u>cautious</u>

4. When there are a large number of things – <u>numerous</u>

5. Another word for beautiful is <u>gorgeous</u>

6. My office is very big and roomy – it's <u>spacious</u>

7. Another word for very, very big – <u>enormous</u>

8. Another word for worried, nervous – <u>anxious</u>

Notes. Write 3 sentences with these '-ous' words.

-ous word search

```
i z l v q j s q s c x m q s o
s v x i o u x u o p e a s q f
j u w y o f o n m x h w u f y
l j o i x r t c k l b c o a j
r u r d e i d s f h c j l m r
s u t g n s u o e g a r u o c
f g n u l e u o j f q h c u s
n a o q j a r o r c u z i s u
d u s k i v m r i m s k d l o
s d e o q q q o o x t g i y i
n f r q z n z r r h n g r u r
f r i v o l o u s o n a y u u
s u o e s u a n b e u n i q c
y f u t s n e r v o u s c s p
s k s n j e s q b b l r o a p
```

anxious	nervous
continuous	serious
courageous	
curious	
dangerous	
famously	
frivolous	
furious	
glamorous	
horrendous	
humorous	
joyous	
nauseous	
ridiculous	

Word Search – Find the words and circle them

```
s k e v y o a c l a d f v w b m g t i f
a e g l t c w c w x w c t s r j n i n y
r e i e i i t z c f t i g e w e p o d l
g v n t l t l n x o s c l w m o c o e e
u e j s i b u p e u m e x s k c p y f t
m i i o b l d y l m v m s h a e l p i a
e h p q i l i u g a e a o s g e i g n r
n c w t s x m b n s r v i d t k u i i a
t a z z n d h t i r e o e i a i h c t p
z y y d o b m g a s n p n i s t b f e e
a q y d p y c b w a n i a k h z i r l s
l g a y s u m z l w f o g r u c j o y b
l u q x e e g l r e f k p n a b a m n g
c w o w r j y v d b y e s s i t u t v u
a c c o m m o d a t i n g k e u e t q a
d e s s a r r a b m e y m t f r g f h n
n v h g j l h b r j c e f m y g d r e l
n o i s a c c o g c v j f d e d p f a k
d r x a r c g v m h q u m w k f h t w r
i r r e l e v a n t r s v m j g n l o w
```

accommodating   accommodation
achieve   achievement
arguing   argument
definitely   indefinitely
embarrassed   embarrassment
irrelevant   relevant
occasion   occasionally
responsibilities   responsibility
separate   separately

Revision. Fill in the missing letters. Check your answers on the next couple of pages.

unaccept__ble	ach__ __vable	unpronounc__ __ble
appl__c__ble	mana__ __able	sens__tively
su__ __in__tly	subs__qu__ntly	strin__ __ __tly
skil__ __ __ __y	appropr__ __t__ly	unfortun__ __ __ly
particul__rly	s__gn__f__cantly	su__ __e__ __fu__ly
negl__g__ble	suscept__ble	infall__ble
feas__ble	respons__ble	forma__ __y
indefin__t__ly	ind__p__nd__ntly	__nconsp__cuous
incomp__t__nc__	omit__ed	admitt__nce
prefer__nce	r__f__rral	__xp__ll__d
exa__ __ __erated	exh__ __ __stive	exist__nce
anx__ous	anxi__ty	just__f__ __ __bly
def__ing	a__ __lication	read__ly
compuls__ry	st__tionary	bur__ __ __ __cratic
entr__pr__n__urial	c__rric__l__ __ __	__cqu__int__nce
procl__m__tion	recla__m	accla__m
pr__val__nt	expla__ __ __	consc__ent__ous
court__ous	metic__lo__s	s__non__mous

197

Do you know how to spell these words now? If not, do the *Look Say Cover Write Check*. And **check** your spelling letter by letter. Or record them and test yourself.

unacceptable	achievable	unpronounceable
applicable	manageable	sensitively
succinctly	subsequently	stringently
skilfully	appropriately	unfortunately
particularly	significantly	successfully
negligible	susceptible	infallible
feasible	responsible	formally
indefinitely	independently	inconspicuous
incompetence	omitted	admittance

preference	referral	expelled
exaggerated	exhaustive	existence
anxious	anxiety	justifiably
defying	application	readily
compulsory	stationary	bureaucratic
entrepreneurial	curriculum	acquaintance
proclamation	reclaim	acclaim
prevalent	explanation	conscientious
courteous	meticulous	synonymous

Notes

Book recommendations:

Spelling Rules Workbook Joanne Rudling
The Reasons Why English Spelling is so Weird and Wonderful
Joanne Rudling (all available from howtospell.co.uk or Amazon)
Spelling Essentials Shireen Shuster (Longman)
A Useful Spelling Handbook for Adults Catherine Taylor (Olympia Publishers)
Signposts to Spelling Joy Pollock (Blessings Book Publishing)
The Complete Guide to English Spelling Rules John J. Fulford (Astoria Press)
The Book of Spelling Rules (Wordsworth Reference)
Any book by David Crystal

For Teachers
Teaching Spelling to English Language Learners relevant to all teachers Johanna Stirling (Amazon) (blog http://thespellingblog.blogspot.co.uk)
Spelling Rules, Riddles and Remedies Sally Raymond (Routledge)
Words their Way Bear, Invernizzi, Templeton, Johnston (Pearson)

Websites
www.howtospell.co.uk
http://www.steveslearning.com/qtsliteracysupport.htm
www.bbc.co.uk/skillswise
www.beatingdyslexia.com

Online Dictionaries (and a big thanks to:)
www.oxforddictionaries.com – British & American & pronunciation
www.macmillandictionary.com – British & American & pronunciation
http://dictionary.cambridge.org British & American & pronunciation
American online dictionary – www.merriam-webster.com

If you have any QTS tips & words,
let me know info@howtospell.co.uk

Notes
Other words

Printed in Great Britain
by Amazon